# 1 MONTH OF
# FREE
# READING

## at

## www.ForgottenBooks.com

---

By purchasing this book you are eligible for one month membership to ForgottenBooks.com, giving you unlimited access to our entire collection of over 1,000,000 titles via our web site and mobile apps.

To claim your free month visit:

www.forgottenbooks.com/free918955

ISBN 978-0-266-98266-1
PIBN 10918955

# FORTY-FIFTH ANNUAL REPORT

OF THE

# a r a. Commissioner of Labor and Statistics. of Maryland 1936

HENRY LAY DUER

Commissioner

16 West Saratoga Street

Baltimore, Maryland

5

Press of
King Bros., Inc.
Baltimore, Md.

# CONTENTS

# CONTENTS

# LETTER OF TRANSMITTAL

———————

To His Excellency,

 Harry W. Nice,

  Governor of Maryland.

Sir:

Pursuant to the requirements of the statute creating this Bureau, I have the honor to submit herewith the forty-fifth annual report of the Commissioner of Labor and Statistics for the year 1936.

Henry Lay Duer,

*Commissioner.*

Baltimore, Maryland, April 17, 1937.

# FORTY-FIFTH ANNUAL REPORT

## OF THE

## COMMISSIONER OF LABOR AND STATISTICS
## MARYLAND

This is the forty-fifth annual report of the Commissioner of Labor and Statistics and covers the activities of the department during the year 1936.

The particular duties of the Commissioner of Labor and Statistics are as follows:

1. To insure compliance with the Labor Laws in just, speedy, and practical ways.

2. To maintain a conciliation service for the convenience of employers and employees in the settlement of labor controversies.

3. To improve industrial relations.

4. To maintain a bureau of general information insofar as is possible.

5. To collect and publish statistics concerning labor and industry in the State.

This report is divided into sections or parts each pertaining to the activities of the several divisions. A brief synopsis of the duties of the various divisions follows:

Division of Conciliation.—This division is called upon to effect agreement between employer and employees in the event of labor disputes and to attempt to avoid resort to lockouts, boycotts, and other discrimination, legal or otherwise, arising out of such controversies.

Division of Statistics.—The duties of this division are to compile and furnish all statistical data needed by this department in the performance of its duties and in its annual report; to furnish also statistical data to all government agencies, labor organizations, employers, schools, and individuals when their requests are reasonable; to maintain a current monthly survey of employment and payrolls in the State.

Children's Division.—Regulation of children in industry is the duty of this division by issuance of employment certificates in compliance with the Child Labor Laws of Maryland; by supervision and issuance of licenses to newsboys and street

traders; by issuance of theatre permits to children in compliance with the law. In connection with this division, and
also in compliance with the law, a medical service is main-
tained for the protection of children entering industry in the
State of Maryland.

Division of Industrial Inspection.—Upon this division falls
the responsibility of enforcing the labor laws of Maryland. Its
duties are manifold and include the inspection of all types of
industrial establishments for sanitation, safety, working conditions, hours of women, child labor, and rules and regulations
for compliance with federal laws. It issues licenses for home
work and workshops. It investigates all complaints and must
issue all correction orders and follow-up orders. The policy of
this division in the past year has been to devote more attention
to places which have possible hazards to life and limb and violations of the labor laws, than to those establishments in which
these conditions seldom prevail.

Division of Boiler Inspection.—This division carries out
the rules and regulations of the Board of Boiler Rules; enforces
the law concerning the inspection of boilers and the issuance
of certificates of inspection of boilers in order to insure greater
safety of such equipment.

Bureau of Mines.—This Bureau is a separate department
under the Commissioner of Labor and Statistics and is charged
with the execution and enforcement of all laws concerning
bituminous coal mines in the State.

The troubled and unsettled period of recovery through which
the country is passing has been responsible for the tremendous
increase in the number of requests for advice, assistance, and
information made upon this department. All requests and inquiries are accorded courteous attention and assistance is
given when possible. But when requests relate to matters outside the scope of this office the applicants are referred to the
proper sources of information. Many of these inquiries are for
unemployment data. Since no current figures on the number
of unemployed are available, estimates have had to be sub-
stituted in many cases. This office recommends that a count
of unemployed persons be taken by some reliable agency in the
very near future as an aid to industry in planning and to government in the administration of relief.

An added burden was placed upon the women of Maryland in
1936 through the recent reversal of the interpretation of the
ten-hour law. It was assumed from an opinion given by the
office of the Attorney General in 1927 that women workers in
restaurants were permitted to work ten hours a day between
the hours of 6 A. M. and 10 P. M. or eight hours a day if any
part of the working time fell in the hours between 10 P. M. and

6 A. ). A recent ruling from the Attorney General's office reversed this opinion and it was found that women restaurant workers were excluded from these restrictions.

As a result of interest in the Walsh-Healey Act passed during the 1936 session of Congress, many inquiries have been made of this office. This measure exercises a decided influence on labor conditions in the country. It gives authority to the Secretary of Labor to set up rules and regulations pertaining to wages, hours, and working conditions of all persons employed directly and indirectly on government contracts, with some few exceptions. Therefore the Federal Department of Labor's regulations and the Act itself become of major importance to practically every employer doing business with the government. In the past, labor conditions were not considered in awarding contracts. By cutting wages and disregarding labor standards many low bids for government contracts were made possible. It was to eliminate such unfair competition that the Walsh-Healey Bill was passed. The passage of this bill is an important step in the improvement of working conditions and will serve as a model for future legislation.

In connection with the investigation of occupational disease conducted in 1936 by the Governor's Commission for the Study of Occupational Diseases, this office contributed the services of seven industrial inspectors for field work in an industrial survey in Maryland. This survey was conducted under the direction of the United States Public Health Service. The personnel was loaned by the Maryland Department of Health, the Baltimore City Department of Health, and the office of the Commissioner of Labor and Statistics. Special interest was centered on potential occupational disease hazards involved in the manufacture of the following products: chemicals and allied products; stone, clay, and glass products; clothing; food and kindred products; iron and steel; machinery; motor vehicles; leather; lumber and allied products; metals, other than iron and steel; paper, printing, and allied products; tobacco; textiles; miscellaneous products. Garages, laundries, dry cleaning establishments, and other industries were also included. A list of approximately 5,000 firms engaged in these industries was assembled in this office and a sample of approximately one-third of the total was thought to be a representative group. The number of plants actually visited was 1,179, 481 of which were investigated by the inspectors loaned by this office. These plants employed 136,422 workers. The inspectors loaned by this office made 40.7 percent of the total number of investigations in the State and 62.0 percent of the total number of investigations made in Baltimore City. The field work lasted six weeks and covered all important industries

in the State. Results of the study have been tabulated and the
final report of factual information on working conditions and
number of persons exposed to occupational disease hazard has
been published by the United States Public Health Service.
This survey is the most extensive study undertaken in the field
of occupational diseases in the United States up to the present
time. It is expected that the findings of this survey will serve
as a basis for recommendations for necessary legislation.

In February 1936 the United States Department of Labor
conducted a ten-day training course for factory inspectors.
The school of hygiene and public health of the Johns Hopkins
University, the Baltimore City Health Department, and the
State Industrial Accident Commission contributed to the success of the program. The majority of the industrial inspectors
of this department attended the course which made an inten-
sive study of safety and sanitation in industrial plants in
Maryland.

The Maryland Unemployment Compensation Law recently
passed by the General Assembly caused deep concern to employers and employees alike by excluding from taxes and bene-
fits the employees of establishments employing fewer than eight
persons. This office was called upon to furnish statistics showing the number of persons affected by this discrimination.

## Recommendations for Legislation

Attention is called to the following recommendations for legislation which this office deems necessary for the good of the
people of Maryland.

Working Hours.—An 8-hour work day and a 48-hour work
week for all employed women, subject to certain exemptions.

Workshops.—A system of fee charging for workshop licenses
to cover cost of printing and mailing, or, the elimination of
these licenses and the substitution in their stead of an effective
sanitation and safety law.

Boiler Inspections.—A revised boiler inspection bill is being
prepared which will include the inspection of unfired vessels.
The present bill can be materially improved upon thereby giving additional revenue to the State with the possibility of making this branch of the department self-supporting and, at the
same time, distributing the fees in such a manner that boiler
owners will not be severely taxed.

Publications.—To amend the law to permit the department
to charge a minimum fee for requested publications and lists,
the fee to cover printing and mailing costs.

Children in Industry.—

1. A minimum age of 16 years for employment in all gainful occupations.

2. Regulations of employment of persons 16 to 18 years of age as follows:

    (a) Hours of work not to exceed 8 hours a day and 40 hours a week, or not to exceed those of adults in the industry in which employed, whichever is the lesser, work to be prohibited between 6 P. M. and 7 A. M.

    (b) Prohibition of employment of persons under 18 years of age in hazardous occupations, the Commissioner of Labor and Statistics to have authority to classify occupations, other than those mentioned in the law, as hazardous for this age group.

    (c) Employment certificates to be required for legal employment of minors between 16 and 18 years of age.

3. Revision of school attendance laws to comply with recommendations for revision of Child Labor Laws.

4. Abolition of industrial homework by children.

January 26, 1937.

## FINANCIAL STATEMENT OF COMMISSIONER OF LABOR AND STATISTICS FOR FISCAL YEAR ENDING SEPTEMBER 30, 1936.

| | Appropriation | Amount Expended | Approximate Amount of Outstanding Bills | Unexpended Balance |
|---|---|---|---|---|
| Total for Salaries.... | $43,373.00 | $43,164.84 | ....... | $ 208.16 |
| Total for Expenses.... | 8,723.00 | 8,253.86 | ....... | 469.14 |
| Grand Total — Salaries and Expenses ...... | $52,096.00 | $51,418.70 | ....... | $ 677.30 |

### SUMMARY

| | | |
|---|---|---|
| Total Appropriation for Salaries and Expenses.......... | | $52,096.00 |
| Total Amount of Salaries and Expenses ... ........... | $51,418.70 | |
| Returned to Board of Public Works, Reserve Fund........ | 677.30 | |

### COLLECTIONS

| | |
|---|---|
| Theatre Permits ........$ | 70.00 |
| Boiler Inspections ...... | 1,560.00 |
| Insurance Companies ... | 924.00 |
| Sale of Used Furniture.. | 4.00 |
| Refund, Credited to Item No. 8 ............... | 10.83 |

| | | |
|---|---|---|
| Total Amount Sent Comptroller ......... | $2,568.83 | |
| Total Amount to be deducted from Appropriation ..........$ | 2,558.00 | |
| Total Amount to be deducted from Appropriation, for Board of Public Works, Reserve Fund | 677.30 | |
| | | 3,235.30 |

Net Expenses of Commissioner of Labor of Statistics......$   48,860.70

Budget Item No. 8—$319.84 held in case of salary claim for Fiscal Year ending September 30, 1935, reverted to State Treasury 3-2-36. (Please see Treas. Dept. Receipt No. 17665.)

# INDUSTRIAL DISPUTES

The year 1936 was marked by serious labor unrest. An unusually large number of strikes and controversies occurred, the majority of which had union recognition and wage increases as major issues. Union recognition figured more largely than wage increases in the strikes. It is to be expected that in this stage of recovery many controversies concerning wages and hours would arise, but greater understanding and an earnest desire to cooperate on the parts of both employer and employee would be important factors in averting strikes with their attendant grief and suffering.

This office was called upon under the Maryland law to render conciliation service in 14 industrial disputes in 1936. In many cases this department worked in cooperation with the Conciliation Service of the United States Department of Labor. In such instances all meetings and conferences were held in this office and negotiations carried on from it.

The following table gives information concerning the strikes in Maryland in 1936 which were handled by the Conciliation Service of the United States Department of Labor. · Those disputes in which this office also participated are marked accordingly.

The general maritime strike for higher wages and better working conditions which started late in October 1936 affected shipping in Baltimore just as it did other Atlantic seaports and the Pacific coast. Approximately 4,800 persons were idle here, either as strikers or because of strike conditions, and shipping was severely crippled. It was terminated in Baltimore on its 87th day—January 25, 1937. The striking groups claimed substantial gains.

On May 4 the dismissal of 5 upholsters by the Chesapeake Manufacturing Company, Baltimore, precipitated a prolonged controversy that was brought to this office for conciliation. The union, Local 75-Upholsterers Union, charged the company with discrimination against union members. The company replied that necessary curtailment of force was the reason for the dismissals. Thirty men were involved directly and indirectly. Adjustment is pending.

In September 1936 approximately 15 furniture upholsterers of the Majestic Furniture Company, Baltimore, gave notice of a threatened strike with union recognition and adjustment of wage rates as the issues involved. On September 21, 1936, through the efforts of this office, a satisfactory agreement was reached with Local 75-Upholsterers Union.

A strike was in progress at the plant of the Celanese Corporation of America, Cumberland, November 12 to December 2, 1936. All 9,000 employees of the company were involved and union recognition and wage increases were the issues. This office was requested to act as conciliator. Agreement was reached with Cumberland Local 1874-United Textile Workers after nearly three weeks of negotiation. Wage increases gained amounted to over $1,250,000 yearly.

On December 31 a controversy developed between employer and employees of the Diamond Taxicab Association, Incorporated caused by the violation of an earlier truce agreement. In connection with conciliation efforts by this office, an investigation of the labor conditions existing in this association was decided upon. The investigation embraces all phases of the

UNITED STATES DEPARTMENT OF LABOR
BUREAU OF LABOR STATISTICS

LABOR DISPUTES HANDLED BY COMMISSIONERS OF CONCILIATION
MARYLAND 1936*

| Company or Industry and Location | Nature of Controversy | Craftsmen Concerned | Cause of Dispute | Present Status and Terms of Settlement | Commissioner Assigned | Assignment Completed | Workers Involved | |
|---|---|---|---|---|---|---|---|---|
| | | | | | | | Directly | Indirectly |
| Foster Bedding Company, Baltimore | Strike | Bedding Workers | Discharges; discrimination alleged | Unclassified. Referred to board of ... more | Jan. 20 | Jan. 24 | 102 | 118 |
| Eastern Rolling Mill Company, Baltimore | Strike | Mill Workers | Proposed wage cut of 10% | Adjusted. Basic rates established; workers returned | Mar. 2 | Mar. 7 | 900 | — |
| Dock Workers, Baltimore | Threatened Strike | Dock Workers | Agreements and working conditions | Adjusted. Strike averted and work continued | Mar. 10 | Mar. 16 | 3,500 | — |
| S.S. Cohen and Sons, Baltimore | Strike | Ladies' Garment Workers | Discharges and refusal to bargain | Unclassified. Referred to National Labor Relations Board | Mar. 11 | Mar. 23 | 53 | — |
| Union Terminal Motor Lines, Incorporated, Baltimore | Strike | Bus Drivers | Asked increases | ... Long ... drivers, increase of $1 per trip; city drivers, increase of $2 per week | May 15 | May 29 | 23 | 6 |
| C and W Motor Lines, Incorporated, Baltimore and other points | Strike | Bus Drivers | Wages and conditions | Adjusted. Satisfactory agreement | May 15 | May 28 | 25 | 10 |
| Eastern Rolling Mill, Baltimore | Strike | Steel Workers | Wages and union recognition | Adjusted. Allowed 13 percent wage increase and union recognition | June 7 | June 24 | 800 | 50 |

| Company | | Workers | Cause | Result | Begun | Ended | | |
|---|---|---|---|---|---|---|---|---|
| George's Transfer and Trucking Company, Incorporated, Baltimore | Strike | Drivers | Wages and union recognition | Adjusted. Wage increase of $3 to $5 per week; all returned | May 11 | June 12 | 35 | 10 |
| †Davidson Transfer Company Baltimore | Strike | Drivers | Wages | Adjusted. Minimum wage for city and road drivers; wage increase of 22½ percent for helpers; all returned | June 13 | June 16 | 250 | 50 |
| Baltimore Drydocks, Baltimore | Strike | Burners and Welders | Asked wage increase and union recognition | Adjusted. Returned on agreement to negotiate differences | June 18 | June 29 | 60 | 940 |
| Maryland Drydock Company, Baltimore | Strike | Burners and Welders | Asked wage increase and union recognition | Adjusted. Returned on agreement to negotiate differences | June 12 | June 29 | 72 | 1,028 |
| †Eastern Rolling Mill, Baltimore | Strike | Iron Steel, and Tin Workers | Asked wage increase and union recognition | Adjusted. Wage increase of 13¼ percent, retroactive to June 1, 1936 | June 12 | June 22 | 800 | 125 |
| †Baltimore Enamel and Novelty Company, Baltimore | Strike | Enamel Workers | Asked wage increase | Adjusted. Wage increases ranging from 20 to 25 percent and reinstatement of those desiring it | May 8 | June 15 | 11 | 439 |
| †Kelly-Springfield Rubber Company, Cumberland | Threatened Strike | Rubber Workers | Wages and discharges | Adjusted. Strike averted at this time | June 14 | July ⁽¹⁾ | 1,352 | 200 |

* Compiled from Monthly Labor Reviews, 1936.

† The Commissioner of Labor and Statistics of Maryland participated in conciliation proceedings.

(1) Not yet reported.

§ Adjusted later by union agreement.

# UNITED STATES DEPARTMENT OF LABOR
## BUREAU OF LABOR STATISTICS

### LABOR DISPUTES HANDLED BY COMMISSIONERS OF CONCILIATION
### MARYLAND 1936*—Continued

| Company or Industry and Location | Nature of Controversy | Craftsmen Concerned | Cause of Dispute | Present Status and Terms of Settlement | Commissioner Assigned | Assignment Completed | | |
|---|---|---|---|---|---|---|---|---|
| †Sonneborn Building, Baltimore | Lock-out | Engineers | Discharge in violation of agreement | Pending | July 13 | — | 4 | — |
| Marshall Transportation Company, Baltimore | Strike | Drivers | Wages | Adjusted. Allowed 30 percent increase and closed-shop agreement | July 10 | July 30 | 13 | 1 |
| Singer Transfer and Storage Company, Baltimore | Strike | Drivers | Wages | Adjusted. Allowed 35 percent increase and closed-shop agreement | July 10 | Aug. 3 | 25 | 4 |
| J. Norman Geipe, Incorporated, Baltimore | Threatened Strike | Truck Drivers | Wage increase | Adjusted. Increase of 30 percent and improved conditions | Aug. 6 | Aug. 7 | 27 | 31 |
| Ericsson Transfer Company, Baltimore | Strike | Drivers | Wages | Adjusted. Increase of 35 percent and closed-shop agreement | Aug. 3 | Aug. 3 | 24 | 12 |
| †Kelly-Springfield Tire Company, Cumberland | Strike | Tire Workers | Wages, union recognition, and reinstatement of those discharged | Adjusted. Union recognized and all returned | Aug. 25 | Sept. 1 | 1,700 | 100 |
| †Calvert Distilling Company, Baltimore | Controversy | Distillery Workers | Wages and working conditions | Pending | Aug. 19 | — | (1) | — |
| M. Shaivitz and Sons Furniture Company, Baltimore | Strike | Teamsters | Wages and union recognition | Pending; returned to work pending negotiations | Aug. 28 | — | 10 | — |
| Abrams and Sons, Incorporated, Baltimore | Strike | Clothing Workers | Wages, union recognition, and closed shop | Pending | Aug. 19 | — | 150 | 10 |

| Establishment | Type | Trade | Cause | Disposition | Begun | Ended | | |
|---|---|---|---|---|---|---|---|---|
| Seidman Transfer Company, Baltimore | Strike | Truck Drivers | Asked 40 percent increase | Adjusted. Satisfactorily settled | Sept. 5 | Sept. 10 | 12 | 18 |
| Deep Seamen, Baltimore | Controversy | Seamen | Insubordination of union member | Adjusted. Settled by seamen's union | June 20 | Sept. 16 | 1 | 100 |
| Shell Eastern Petroleum Company, Baltimore | Strike | Truck Drivers | Union recognition and wage increase | Pending | Sept. 5 | —— | 8 | 50 |
| Oelrich Transfer Company, Baltimore | Threatened Strike | Truck Drivers | Union recognition and wage increase | Pending | Sept. 11 | —— | 30 | 14 |
| †Stone Upholstering Company, Baltimore | Strike | Upholsterers | Wage increase | Adjusted. Increase of 10 percent; returned without discrimination | Sept. 23 | Oct. 16 | 20 | 5 |
| Seamen and Longshoremen, Baltimore | Strike | Ship Workers | New agreement with wage increase | Adjusted. Increases ranging from $10 to $20 per month | Oct. 10 | Oct. 17 | 1,700 | 1,000 |
| Charlton and Brothers Transportation Company, Hagerstown | Strike | Drivers | Union recognition | Adjusted. Satisfactory agreement | Oct. 15 | Oct. 16 | 18 | 2 |
| Automobile Transport Industry, Baltimore | Controversy | Drivers | Wages, hours, and working conditions | Agreed to arbitrate. Local 355-brotherhood teamsters, chauffeurs, stablemen, and helpers | Nov. 9 | Nov. 16 | 1,200 | 3,000 |
| Greenbelt Project, Resettlement Administration, Berwyn | Controversy | Plasterers | Discrimination against non-union plasterers | Satisfactory agreement | Dec. | Dec. 18 | 28 | 4.972 |
| †Diamond Taxicab Association, Baltimore | Strike | Drivers | Discharge of drivers | Adjusted. All those discharged were reinstated pending negotiations | Dec. 17 | Dec. 21 | 800 | 30 |

* Compiled from Monthly Labor Reviews, 1936.
† The Commissioner of Labor and Statistics of Maryland participated in conciliation proceedings.
(1) Not yet reported.
§ Adjusted later by union agreement.

dispute and will include individual testimony from the employers and approximately 900 owner operators and driver operators of the company. The investigation has not been completed at the time of this writing.

## DIVISION OF INDUSTRIAL INSPECTION

The following tables show the number and kinds of inspections made during 1936 and also the number of persons involved by industry, sex, and color, by occupation, and by daily
hours of work. In addition to these inspections, 369 regular
reinspections were made, 224 homeworker licenses were issued,
and 1,863 workshop licenses were issued in Maryland. Orders
for correction of sanitary and safety conditions were issued to
101 firms. Splendid cooperation from employers in the correction of faulty working conditions has been accorded this division.

NUMBER OF FIRST INSPECTIONS MADE BY THE INDUSTRIAL
INSPECTORS IN 1936

| State and Political Sub-division | Number of Establishments | Child Labor | Ten-Hour Law | Factory | General | Total Number of Inspections |
|---|---|---|---|---|---|---|
| State. . . . . . . . . . . . . . . | 21,063 | 196 | 5,840 | 1,296 | 15,085 | 22,417 |
| Baltimore City . . . . . . . . | 15,172 | 112 | 4,260 | 1,073 | 10,844 | 16,289 |
| Allegany County . . . . . . | 1 | ... | 1 | ... | ... | 1 |
| Anne Arundel County.. | 696 | ... | 170 | 30 | 526 | 726 |
| Baltimore County . . . . . | 487 | 5 | 173 | 23 | 311 | 512 |
| Calvert County . . . . . . . . | 82 | ... | 15 | ... | 67 | 82 |
| Caroline County . . . . . . . | 302 | 18 | 71 | 10 | 213 | 312 |
| Carroll County . . . . . . . . | 179 | 4 | 61 | 14 | 115 | 194 |
| Cecil County . . . . . . . . . . | 279 | ... | 78 | 4 | 201 | 283 |
| Charles County . . . . . . . . | 70 | 1 | 13 | 2 | 56 | 72 |
| Dorchester County . . . . | 455 | 16 | 112 | 20 | 327 | 475 |
| Frederick County . . . . . | 107 | 1 | 60 | 10 | 47 | 118 |
| Harford County . . . . . . . | 354 | 1 | 90 | 11 | 264 | 366 |
| Howard County . . . . . . . | 45 | 1 | 21 | 3 | 24 | 49 |
| Kent County . . . . . . . . . . | 242 | 3 | 63 | 4 | 176 | 246 |
| Prince George's County. | 681 | 2 | 155 | 10 | 526 | 693 |
| Queen Anne's County.. | 213 | 4 | 39 | 3 | 173 | 219 |
| St. Mary's County. . . . . . | 104 | ... | 13 | 2 | 91 | 106 |
| Somerset County . . . . . . | 371 | 3 | 91 | 7 | 277 | 378 |
| Talbot County . . . . . . . . | 331 | 6 | 83 | 10 | 242 | 341 |
| Washington County . . . | 18 | 1 | 12 | 12 | 5 | 30 |
| Wicomico County . . . . . . | 602 | 8 | 167 | 38 | 428 | 641 |
| Worcester County . . . . . | 272 | 10 | 92 | 10 | 172 | 284 |

| | 21,063 | 166,103 | 27,625 | 71,620 | 11,166 | 15,172 | 120,976 | 15,485 | 52,036 |
|---|---|---|---|---|---|---|---|---|---|
| All Industries | | | | | | | | | |
| Manufacturing industries | 2 570 | 83,349 | 16,605 | 40,147 | 8,860 | 1,834 | 52,351 | 6,382 | 24,915 |
| Chemicals | 139 | 6,011 | 1,891 | 819 | 13 | 120 | 5,845 | 1,765 | 770 |
| Distilled products | 28 | 1,196 | 55 | 894 | 2 | 21 | 617 | 29 | 585 |
| Food products | 626 | 13,066 | 5,291 | 8 038 | 7,947 | 261 | 8,655 | 839 | 3,642 |
| Canning, vegetables | 161 | 3,609 | 3,464 | 4,742 | 6,536 | 16 | 703 | 66 | 1,148 |
| Canning, seafood | 116 | 763 | 1,042 | 768 | 1,387 | 7 | 81 | 121 | 24 |
| Other food products | 346 | 8,694 | 785 | 2,528 | 24 | 238 | 7,871 | 652 | 2,470 |
| Iron and steel | 138 | 19,961 | 6,121 | 1,850 | 152 | 125 | 7,775 | 898 | 1,567 |
| Leather products | 29 | 1,147 | 96 | 857 | 1 | 25 | 768 | 96 | 500 |
| Lumber | 155 | 3,081 | 438 | 264 | 23 | 106 | 2,254 | 221 | 152 |
| Machinery | 31 | 1,844 | 103 | 233 | .... | 26 | 1,128 | 97 | 59 |
| Metal products, other than iron and steel | 62 | 4,002 | 639 | 582 | 1 | 61 | 3,949 | 639 | 581 |
| Paper and printing | 325 | 5,656 | 208 | 1,497 | 20 | 252 | 4,817 | 200 | 1,401 |
| Stone, clay, and glass products | 68 | 2,171 | 902 | 322 | 29 | 39 | 2,023 | 790 | 311 |
| Textiles | 571 | 14,615 | 360 | 22,429 | 647 | 474 | 6,889 | 354 | 13,370 |
| Clothing, men's and boys' | 368 | 4,200 | 161 | 7,034 | 139 | 271 | 3,900 | 157 | 5,154 |
| Clothing, men's and women's | 5 | 60 | 5 | 415 | .... | 4 | 58 | 5 | 414 |
| Clothing, women's and children's | 93 | 797 | 58 | 3,174 | 116 | 80 | 755 | 58 | 2,717 |
| Furnishings, men's | 36 | 382 | 12 | 2,793 | 121 | 29 | 355 | 12 | 2,221 |

NUMBER OF PERSONS FOUND EMPLOYED BY INDUSTRIAL INSPECTORS IN THE STATE AND BALTIMORE CITY IN 1936, BY INDUSTRY IN WHICH EMPLOYED, COLOR, AND SEX—(Continued)

| Industry | State | | | | | Baltimore City | | | | |
|---|---|---|---|---|---|---|---|---|---|---|
| | Number of Establishments | Male White | Male Colored | Female White | Female Colored | Number of Establishments | Male White | Male Colored | Female White | Female Colored |
| Hats and caps | 18 | 311 | 13 | 353 | 3 | 18 | 311 | 13 | 353 | 3 |
| Millinery | 5 | 59 | 10 | 133 | .. | 5 | 59 | 10 | 133 | .. |
| Shirts and overalls | 46 | 539 | 36 | 3,358 | 181 | 22 | 417 | 34 | 1,339 | 181 |
| Other textiles | 60 | 8,267 | 65 | 5,169 | 87 | 45 | 1,034 | 65 | 1039 | 87 |
| Tobacco | 14 | 54 | 2 | 122 | 2 | 12 | 48 | 2 | 120 | 2 |
| Transportation equipment | 30 | 5,012 | 36 | 143 | .. | 22 | 3,234 | 35 | 97 | .. |
| Miscellaneous manufacturing | 354 | 5,533 | 463 | 2,097 | 23 | 290 | 4,349 | 417 | 1,760 | 20 |
| Building industries | 1,847 | 746 | 1,670 | 444 | 2 | 1,366 | 5,495 | 1,298 | 386 | 1 |
| Building | 57 | 780 | 323 | 34 | .. | 51 | 678 | 318 | 32 | .. |
| Electrical contracting | 34 | 223 | 1 | 18 | .. | 21 | 177 | 1 | 11 | .. |
| General contracting | 43 | 1,574 | 910 | 37 | .. | 40 | 1,132 | 650 | 30 | .. |
| Painting | 16 | 51 | .. | 2 | .. | 8 | 36 | .. | 2 | .. |
| Paperhanging | 25 | 49 | 1 | 5 | .. | 25 | 49 | 1 | 5 | .. |
| Plumbing and heating | 146 | 674 | 36 | 51 | .. | 119 | 540 | 15 | 42 | .. |
| Roofing | 37 | 283 | 48 | 12 | .. | 26 | 250 | 48 | 11 | .. |
| Miscellaneous mechanical industries | 1,489 | 3,412 | 351 | 285 | 2 | 1,076 | 2,633 | 265 | 253 | 1 |
| Mercantile establishments | 10,342 | 29,337 | 2,932 | 18,178 | 395 | 7,100 | 20,650 | 2,245 | 15,576 | 352 |
| Auto sales and service | 287 | 2,713 | 299 | 208 | .. | 109 | 1,501 | 171 | 123 | .. |
| Radio sales and service | 36 | 92 | 3 | 13 | .. | 19 | 49 | 2 | 8 | .. |

## NUMBER OF PERSONS FOUND EMPLOYED BY INDUSTRIAL INSPECTORS IN THE STATE AND BALTIMORE CITY IN 1936, BY INDUSTRY IN WHICH EMPLOYED, COLOR, AND SEX—(Continued)

| Industry | State | | | | | Baltimore City | | | | |
|---|---|---|---|---|---|---|---|---|---|---|
| | Number of Establishments | Male White | Male Colored | Female White | Female Colored | Number of Establishments | Male White | Male Colored | Female White | Female Colored |
| Retail department stores | 91 | 3,474 | 253 | 7,649 | 76 | 39 | 3,252 | 248 | 7,362 | 76 |
| Retail limited-price stores | 87 | 233 | 35 | 1,187 | 12 | 49 | 170 | 33 | 975 | 12 |
| Wholesale stores | 983 | 3,509 | 293 | 1,733 | 102 | 819 | 2,684 | 243 | 1,676 | 102 |
| Wholesale and retail stores | 284 | 1566 | 252 | 280 | 4 | 262 | 1,426 | 237 | 263 | 4 |
| Offices | 543 | 4,329 | 447 | 2,105 | 63 | 471 | 3,938 | 398 | 1,925 | 63 |
| Professional | 129 | 281 | 17 | 62 | 5 | 126 | 274 | 17 | 62 | 5 |
| Public utilities | 342 | 31,755 | 2,716 | 4,409 | 19 | 193 | 30,635* | 2,557* | 4,322* | 15* |
| Service trades | 5,138 | 9,305 | 3,067 | 6,218 | 1,820 | 3,942 | 7,130 | 2,462 | 4,794 | 1,530 |
| Amusements | 156 | 520 | 430 | 65 | 20 | 85 | 334 | 335 | 56 | 18 |
| Barber shops | 951 | 1,403 | 349 | 28 | 5 | 676 | 986 | 272 | 24 | 5 |
| Beauty shops | 515 | 59 | 5 | 968 | 209 | 409 | 47 | 4 | 748 | 191 |
| Cleaning and pressing | 816 | 1,266 | 459 | 443 | 120 | 679 | 1,024 | 355 | 380 | 101 |
| Hotels | 26 | 688 | 224 | 443 | 61 | 18 | 659 | 221 | 408 | 60 |
| Laundries | 245 | 1,245 | 212 | 1,299 | 693 | 199 | 951 | 191 | 925 | 642 |
| Restaurants, cafeterias, and eating places | 2,303 | 3,764 | 1,287 | 2,869 | 699 | 1,751 | 2,769 | 985 | 2,150 | 500 |
| Bus service trades | 126 | 360 | 101 | 103 | 13 | 125 | 360 | 99 | 103 | 13 |
| Other establishments | 152 | 701 | ·171 | 57 | 2 | 140 | 503 | 126 | 56 | 2 |

* May include some persons employed outside Baltimore City, employed by organizations submitting reports for entire State.

NUMBER OF MEN FOUND EMPLOYED BY INDUSTRIAL INSPECTORS IN THE STATE AND BALTIMORE CITY IN 1936, BY OCCUPATION, INDUSTRY, AND COLOR

| Occupation | White | | | | | | | | |
|---|---|---|---|---|---|---|---|---|---|
| | All Industries | Manufacturing | Mechanical | Mercantile | Offices | Professional | Public Utilities | Service Trades | Other Establishments |
| State | 166,103 | 83,349 | 7,046 | 29,337 | 4,329 | 281 | 31,755 | 9,305 | 701 |
| Office | 20,998 | 7,105 | 652 | 2,655 | 2,257 | 127 | 7,679 | 408 | 115 |
| Sales | 30,887 | 4,475 | 257 | 17,728 | 1,436 | 5 | 3,126 | 3,811 | 49 |
| Workroom | 80,681 | 66,924 | 3,597 | 3,902 | 87 | 49 | 3,445 | 2,515 | 162 |
| Domestic | 605 | 98 | 29 | 93 | 60 | ... | 5 | 320 | ... |
| Other | 32,932 | 4,747 | 2,511 | 4,959 | 489 | 100 | 17,500 | 2,251 | 375 |
| Baltimore City | 120,976 | 52,351 | 5,495 | 20,650 | 3,938 | 274 | 30,635* | 7,130 | 503 |
| Office | 18,244 | 5,453 | 584 | 2,138 | 2,031 | 124 | 7,464 | 340 | 110 |
| Sales | 22,750 | 3,739 | 222 | 11,435 | 1,396 | 5 | 3,099 | 2,805 | 49 |
| Workroom | 49,796 | 38,821 | 2,681 | 2,684 | 78 | 48 | 3,298 | 2,044 | 142 |
| Domestic | 517 | 94 | 28 | 93 | 60 | ... | 5 | 237 | ... |
| Other | 29,669 | 4,244 | 1,980 | 4,300 | 373 | 97 | 16,769 | 1,704 | 202 |

* May include some persons employed outside Baltimore City, employed by organizations submitting reports for entire State.

## NUMBER OF MEN FOUND EMPLOYED BY INDUSTRIAL INSPECTORS IN THE STATE AND BALTIMORE CITY IN 1936, BY OCCUPATION, INDUSTRY, AND COLOR

| Occupation | Colored | | | | | | | | |
|---|---|---|---|---|---|---|---|---|---|
| | All Industries | Manufacturing | Mechanical | Mercantile | Offices | Professional | Public Utilities | Service Trades | Other Establishments |
| State | 27,625 | 6,605 | 1,670 | 2,932 | 447 | 17 | 2,716 | 3,067 | 171 |
| Office | 101 | 42 | 1 | 18 | 17 | 3 | 4 | 14 | 2 |
| Sales | 1,046 | 10 | 4 | 336 | 304 | | ... | 390 | 2 |
| Workroom | 17,325 | 15,226 | 289 | 438 | 5 | 1 | 289 | 1,056 | 21 |
| Domestic | 900 | 71 | 8 | 232 | 3 | ... | 70 | 515 | 1 |
| Other | 8,253 | 1,256 | 1,368 | 1,908 | 118 | 13 | 2,353 | 1,092 | 145 |
| Baltimore City | 15,485 | 6,382 | 1,298 | 2,245 | 398 | 17 | 2,557* | 2,462 | 126 |
| Office | 84 | 35 | 1 | 9 | 17 | 3 | 3 | 14 | 2 |
| Sales | 813 | 10 | 4 | 234 | 304 | | ... | 259 | 2 |
| Workroom | 6,638 | 5,130 | 188 | 211 | 5 | 1 | 172 | 910 | 21 |
| Domestic | 766 | 64 | 8 | 217 | 3 | ... | 70 | 403 | 1 |
| Other | 7,184 | 1,143 | 1,097 | 1,574 | 69 | 13 | 2,312 | 876 | 100 |

* May include some persons employed outside Baltimore City, employed by organizations submitting reports for entire State.

NUMBER OF WOMEN FOUND EMPLOYED BY INDUSTRIAL INSPECTORS IN THE STATE AND BALTIMORE CITY 1936, BY OCCUPATION, INDUSTRY, AND COLOR

| Occupation | White | | | | | | | | |
| --- | --- | --- | --- | --- | --- | --- | --- | --- | --- |
| | All Industries | Manufacturing | Mechanical | Mercantile | Offices | Professional | Public Utilities | Service Trades | Other Establishments |
| State | 71,620 | 40,147 | 444 | 18,178 | 2,105 | 62 | 4,409 | 6,218 | 57 |
| Office | 2,911 | 3,565 | 273 | 4,295 | 1,973 | 55 | 2,234 | 486 | 30 |
| Sales | 14,823 | 884 | 24 | 11,419 | 32 | 1 | 33 | 2,428 | 2 |
| Workroom | 8,264 | 35,476 | 142 | 841 | 18 | 1 | 34 | 2,233 | 19 |
| Domestic | 715 | 125 | ... | 90 | 63 | ... | 66 | 371 | ... |
| Other | 4,407 | 97 | 5 | 1,533 | 19 | 5 | 2,042 | 700 | 6 |
| Baltimore City | 52,036 | 24,915 | 386 | 15,576 | 1,925 | 62 | 4,322* | 4,794 | 56 |
| Office | 11,499 | 2,990 | 230 | 3,833 | 1,797 | 55 | 2,147 | 418 | 29 |
| Sales | 12,065 | 825 | 15 | 9,339 | 32 | 1 | 33 | 1,818 | 2 |
| Workroom | 23,625 | 20,886 | 136 | 794 | 17 | 1 | 34 | 1,738 | 19 |
| Domestic | 653 | 124 | ... | 83 | 63 | ... | 66 | 317 | ... |
| Other | 4,194 | 90 | 5 | 1,527 | 16 | 5 | 2,042 | 503 | 6 |

* May include some persons employed outside Baltimore City, employed by organizations submitting reports for entire State.

NUMBER OF WOMEN FOUND EMPLOYED BY INDUSTRIAL INSPECTORS IN THE STATE AND BALTIMORE CITY 1936, BY OCCUPATION, INDUSTRY, AND COLOR

| Occupation | Colored | | | | | | | | |
|---|---|---|---|---|---|---|---|---|---|
| | All Industries | Manufacturing | Mechanical | Mercantile | Offices | Professional | Public Utilities | Service Trades | Other Establishments |
| State | 11,166 | 8,860 | 2 | 395 | 63 | 5 | 19 | 1,820 | 2 |
| Office | 48 | 15 | ... | 1 | 26 | ... | ... | 6 | ... |
| Sales | 355 | 8 | ... | 97 | 17 | ... | ... | 233 | ... |
| Workroom | 9,837 | 8,801 | 2 | 90 | ... | ... | 7 | 937 | ... |
| Domestic | 444 | 10 | ... | 68 | 10 | ... | 3 | 353 | ... |
| Other | 482 | 26 | ... | 139 | 10 | 5 | 9 | 291 | 2 |
| Baltimore City | 2,915 | 947 | 1 | 352 | 63 | 5 | 15* | 1,530 | 2 |
| Office | 47 | 15 | ... | ... | 26 | ... | ... | 6 | ... |
| Sales | 270 | 8 | ... | 70 | 17 | ... | ... | 175 | ... |
| Workroom | 1,854 | 892 | 1 | 90 | ... | ... | 7 | 864 | ... |
| Domestic | 286 | 7 | ... | 54 | 10 | ... | ... | 215 | ... |
| Other | 458 | 25 | ... | 138 | 10 | 5 | 8 | 270 | 2 |

* May include some persons employed outside Baltimore City, employed by organizations submitting reports for entire State.

NUMBER OF WOMEN FOUND EMPLOYED BY INDUSTRIAL INSPECTORS IN THE STATE AND BALTIMORE CITY IN 1936, BY NUMBER OF HOURS WORKED DAILY AND INDUSTRY IN WHICH EMPLOYED

| Hours Worked Daily | All Industries | Manufacturing Industries | Mechanical Industries | Mercantile Industries | Offices | Professional | Public Utilities | Service Trades | Other Establishments |
|---|---|---|---|---|---|---|---|---|---|
| State | 82,786 | 49,007 | 446 | 18,573 | 2,168 | 67 | 4,428 | 8,038 | 59 |
| Less than eight hours | 21,757 | 9,272 | 214 | 8,481 | 1,793 | 38 | 353 | 1,588 | 18 |
| Eight hours | 28,522 | 9,041 | 147 | 4,610 | 329 | 20 | 1,395 | 2,351 | 29 |
| Eight hours—less than nine hours | 7,014 | 2,846 | 12 | 459 | ... | ... | 2,665 | 1,032 | ... |
| Nine hours—less than ten hours | 5,405 | 3,426 | 1 | 902 | 1 | 1 | 3 | 1,071 | ... |
| Ten hours | 790 | 513 | 4 | 64 | ... | ... | 4 | 205 | ... |
| *More than ten hours | 37 | 1 | ... | 10 | ... | ... | ... | 26 | ... |
| *Hours unreported | 19,261 | 13,308 | 68 | 4,047 | 45 | 8 | 8 | 1,765 | 12 |
| Baltimore City | 54,951 | 25,862 | 387 | 15,928 | 1,988 | 67 | 4,337† | 6,324 | 58 |
| Less than eight hours | 19,284 | 8,000 | 179 | 7,814 | 1,694 | 38 | 281 | 1,261 | 17 |
| Eight hours | 20,459 | 12,921 | 142 | 3,895 | 250 | 20 | 1,383 | 1,819 | 29 |
| Eight hours—less than nine hours | 5,973 | 2,115 | 12 | 311 | ... | ... | 2,665 | 870 | ... |
| Nine hours—less than ten hours | 2,759 | 1,235 | ... | 758 | ... | 1 | ... | 765 | ... |
| Ten hours | 621 | 479 | ... | 19 | ... | ... | ... | 123 | ... |
| *More than ten hours | 33 | 1 | ... | 8 | ... | ... | ... | 24 | ... |
| *Hours unreported | 5,822 | 1, 1 | 54 | 3,123 | 44 | 8 | 8 | 1,462 | 12 |

* Includes workers in canneries, women proprietors, and other women workers not covered by the laws governing the hours of employment of women.

† May include some persons employed outside Baltimore City, employed by organizations submitting reports for the entire State.

The figures in the foregoing tables concerning women in industry include those who come within the jurisdiction of the laws governing the hours of labor for women and those who do not. As the following tables indicate the greatest number of women was found employed in manufacturing industries and the largest single group of women worked eight hours a day.

| Industry | Percent of Women | |
|---|---|---|
| | State | Baltimore City |
| All industries ........................ | 100.0 | 100.0 |
| Manufacturing industries .............. | 59.2 | 47.1 |
| Mechanical industries ................ | 0.5 | 0.7 |
| Mercantile industries ................. | 22.4 | 29.0 |
| Offices.... ............................ | 2.6 | 3.6 |
| Professional... ....................... | 0.1 | 0.1 |
| Public Utilities ...................... | 5.4 | 7.9 |
| Service trades ....................... | 9.7 | 11.5 |
| Other establishments ................. | 0.1 | 0.1 |

| Number of Hours Worked Daily | Percent of Women | |
|---|---|---|
| | State | Baltimore City |
| Less than eight hours................. | 26.3 | 35.1 |
| Eight hours ......................... | 34.4 | 37.2 |
| Eight hours—less than nine hours..... | 8.5 | 10.9 |
| Nine hours—less than ten hours....... | 6.5 | 5.0 |
| Ten hours ........ ................... | 0.9 | 1.1 |
| *More than ten hours................. | 0.1 | 0.1 |
| *Hours not reported.................. | 23.3 | 10.6 |

* Includes workers in canneries, women proprietors, and other women workers not covered by the laws governing the hours of employment of women.

Reports of 261 violations in 71 establishments of the laws governing the hours of employment of women were made by the industrial inspectors in Maryland during 1936. The working hours of all the women involved in these cases were changed to comply with the law and schedules posted on the premises accordingly.

Violations of the child labor laws were reported for 167 establishments involving 234 children. Details of these violations appear elsewhere in this report. The following table shows the distribution of these violations by location:

| County | Number of Establishments | Number of Children |
|---|---|---|
| Baltimore City ................. | 122 | 144 |
| Baltimore.... ................... | 5 | 16 |
| Caroline.... ................... | 9 | 23 |
| Carroll.... .................... | 4 | 9 |
| Charles.... .................... | 1 | 1 |
| Dorchester.... ................. | 7 | 10 |
| Harford..... ................... | 1 | 2 |
| Kent........................... | 1 | 1 |
| Prince George's ............... | 2 | 2 |
| Somerset.... ................... | 2 | 12 |
| Talbot.... .................... | 5 | 5 |
| Washington.... ................. | 1 | 1 |
| Wicomico.... ................... | 4 | 5 |
| Worcester.... .................. | 3 | 3 |
| Total.............. | 167 | 234 |

In 1936 nine cases of occupational diseases were reported to this office by the State Department of Health; 5 cases involved lead poisoning and 4 cases involved dermatitis.

### Free Employment Service

The department conducts a free employment service. Seven hundred four new applicants for employment registered with this department during 1936; 1,119 applicants were referred to employers, 407 of these were verified placements. This includes both temporary and permanent positions. Because of a limited communications-budget, it was impossible to verify results of referrals of many more individuals from whom this office has not had follow-up information.

## CHILDREN'S DIVISION

Before discussing the past year's work, it may be interesting to review very briefly the steps that have been taken by the State of Maryland to protect her working children during the last quarter of a century. Twenty-five years ago the General Assembly passed "a modern child labor law"—the first thorough child labor law that had been enacted for the State. This law became effective December 1, 1912 and prohibited the employment of children under 14 years of age in practically all employments except domestic service or agricultural work. The law provided for the certification of all children leaving school to engage in strictly industrial pursuits. Certain dangerous or injurious occupations were prohibited to children under 16 years of age and between the ages of 16 and 18 years. In 1916 the law was amended to provide still greater protection to employed children and to prevent children under 14 years of age from withdrawing from school to enter industry. Hours of work for children under 16 years of age were limited to 8 hours a day, 48 hours a week. Night work was prohibited to minors under 16 years.

Since that time the law has remained practically unaltered in spite of the fact that a decided change in industrial conditions has taken place in the years that have followed. There has been a general raising of standards and in many cases adults are working under more favorable conditions than are required by law for our 14 and 15 year old children. The Department feels that our present child labor standards should be reviewed and redrafted by authorities on school and labor problems in order to protect children against the strains and hazards that are still part of our industrial system.

At the Third National Conference on Labor Legislation held in Washington, D. C. in November 1936, the Committee on Child Labor Standards made the following recommendations which were adopted unanimously:

"State Legislation: We heartily commend all efforts by States to improve the standards of their child labor laws and urge that every effort be made to incorporate in all State child-labor laws the following standards:

1. A minimum age of 16 years for employment in all gainful occupations, including industrialized agriculture away from the home farm.

2. The regulation of employment of young persons 16 to 18 years of age, as follows:

(a) Hours of work not to exceed 8 hours per day and 40 hours per week; or not to exceed those of adults in the industry in which employed, whichever is the lesser. Night work to be prohibited between 6 P. M. and 7 A. M.

(b) Prohibition of employment of persons under 18 in hazardous occupations, the State Department of Labor or industrial board to have authority to classify occupations as hazardous for this age group.

(c) Employment certificates to be required for the legal employment of minors under 18 years of age.

School Attendance: We urge that every effort be made to revise upward our State school attendance laws to conform with the higher minimum age and employment certificate requirements recommended for State child-labor laws and to emphasize also the need for the provision by

tie schools of an enriched and varied school program to
meet tie needs of all young people.

Industrial Home Work: We wish to emphasize our conviction tiat industrial iome work, tiat is, tie sending of
factory work to be done in tie iome, serves not only to
exploit tie ciild worker but also to break down labor
standards in general tirougi tie reintroduction of tie
sweatsiop, and urge tierefore tie speedy enactment of
legislation looking to its abolition."

Tiese recommendations are in line witi tie NRA codes
wiich eliminated from industry tie employment of ciildren
under 16 years of age during school iours. Witi tie decrease
of ciild workers under 16 years of age, tie unemployed young
people between 16 and 18 years iad an opportunity to secure
jobs wiile tie younger ciildren were attending school. As soon
as tie NRA codes were invalidated, tiere was an increase in
child labor. In November 1936 tie Ciildren's Bureau issued a
bulletin comparing tie number of employment certificates
issued to 14 and 15 year old ciildren in tie first five montis of
1935, wien tie ciild labor provisions of tie NRA were still in
effect, witi tiose issued in tie same period in 1936. Tie figures
covered ten States wiere no cianges in tie ciild labor laws
iad been made, tie District of Columbia, and 98 cities in otier
States. Tiey revealed an increase of 150 percent in tie number issued during tie 1936 period compared witi tie number
issued in 1935—8,400 compared witi 3,350. Maryland was included in tiis study.

In 1936 tiere was a large increase in tie number of applicants interviewed for employment certificates and in tie number of employment certificates issued. Tie summary following
gives information on tie certificates issued and refused:

## Baltimore City

*Employment Certificates Issued:*

In Baltimore City in 1936, 1,455 employment certificates
were issued to ciildren under 16 years of age. Of tiis number,
399 were regular certificates, 386 vacation certificates, and 670
vocational or "special" certificates. Wien compared witi tie
number issued in 1935, tiis represents an increase of 78.3 percent. Tiis increase is attributable partly, no doubt, to tie increase in employment in all age groups and to tie invalidation
of tie NRA.

Of tie 399 regular certificates issued, 355 were first regular
certificates—ciildren who iad severed tieir connection witi
sciool and entered tie ranks of industry for tie first time.

Forty-four were subsequent regular certificates — issued to children under 16 years who changed their employment. Of the 386 vacation certificates, 365 were first vacation certificates and 21 were subsequent vacation certificates. Of the 670 vocational or "special" certificates, 203 were first vocational and 467 were either subsequent or renewed certificates.

In considering the children who secured employment certificates, it will be noticed that the number of colored children, 48, who secured certificates, is unusually small, both in proportion to the number of white children and to the colored population of the city. This may be due to two reasons: (1) many colored girls are employed in domestic service for which the law does not require certificates; (2) colored children in industry have never received the special attention that is required, if they are to be protected as the law provides. When we learn from the Department of Education that over 300 colored boys between the ages of 14 and 16 years left school from February 1936 to June 1936, and that only 48 can be accounted for through this division, we naturally wonder what these children are doing. Are they in idleness on the streets? Are they going into less well regulated and less desirable occupations, working long hours and under unfavorable conditions?

## Refused Certificates:

During the year 76 children were refused employment certificates—27 regular and 49 vacation certificates. Of these children, 66 were white boys, 5 colored boys, and 5 white girls.

## Reasons for Refusal:

Twenty-seven children were refused first regular certificates for the following reasons: 2 white boys were under the legal age of 14 years; 13 white boys, 1 colored boy, and 1 white girl had secured work in occupations forbidden by the law; 9 white boys and 1 colored boy had secured work in occupations requiring more than 8 hours work a day or before 7 A. M. or after 7 P. M. Of the 49 vacation certificates refused, 33 white boys, 1 colored boy, and 2 white girls were under the age of 14; 6 white boys, 1 colored boy, and 1 white girl had secured work in forbidden occupations; 3 white boys, 1 colored boy, and 1 white girl had secured work in occupations requiring more than 8 hours work a day.

## Place of Birth:

As usual, by far the largest group who secured first regular and vacation certificates in Baltimore during 1936 had been born in Baltimore City. While 82.5 percent of 720 children were in this group, the next largest group, 9.2 percent, had been born in other States.

## Evidence of Age:

Age is still the fundamental basis of all child labor legislation in this country and before allowing a child to enter industry we must have proof that he is actually 14 years of age. In 1936, 71.4 percent of all first regular and vacation certificates were issued upon receipt of official birth records and passports and 24.0 percent upon baptismal certificates. In other words, 95.4 percent of all first regular and vacation certificates secured by children during the year were issued upon some documentary evidence of age. Only 33 first regular and vacation certificates, or 4.6 percent, were issued upon affidavits of parents.

## Grade Completed:

In 1929 the General Assembly of Maryland raised the minimum grade requirement for the general certification of children to the completion of the course prescribed by the elementary schools, which in Baltimore City is equivalent to the completion of the 6th grade. In view of this fact, it is interesting to review the distribution of those children who secured first regular employment certificates in Baltimore during each of the last several years by last grade completed:

Percent

| Last Grade Completed. | 1936 | 1935 | 1934 | 1933 | 1932 | 1931 | 1930 | 1929 | 1928 | 1927 |
|---|---|---|---|---|---|---|---|---|---|---|
| Total. . . . . . | 100.0 | 100.0 | 100.0 | 100.0 | 100.0 | 100.0 | 100.0 | 100.0 | 100.0 | 100.0 |
| Fifth. . . .. | ... | ... | ... | ... | ... | ... | 0.6 | 7.1 | 10.2 | 12.3 |
| Sixth. . . . . | 34.1 | 27.7 | 43.8 | 29.4 | 37.3 | 32.6 | 31.2 | 28.1 | 22.6 | 23.4 |
| Seventh. . . | 31.8 | 33.8 | 18.8 | 31.4 | 28.6 | 32.5 | 33.7 | 33.1 | 32.0 | 29.8 |
| Eighth. . .. | 21.7 | 26.3 | 18.8 | 28.8 | 24.8 | 25.6 | 22.7 | 22.8 | 25.0 | 25.5 |
| Ninth. . . . . | 9.6 | 9.5 | 6.2 | 9.0 | 8.6 | 7.8 | 10.4 | 7.8 | 9.0 | 6.4 |
| Tenth. . . . | 2.8 | 2.0 | 6.2 | 1.1 | 0.5 | 1.3 | 1.4 | 1.1 | 0.9 | ⎫ |
| Eleventh . . | ... | ... | 6.2 | 0.3 | 0.2 | 0.2 | ... | * | 0.2 | ⎬ 2.6 |
| Twelfth. . . | ... | 0.7 | ... | ... | ... | ... | * | * | 0.1 | ⎭ |

*Less than one-tenth of one percent.

## Nativity of Fathers:

Of the 720 children who secured first regular and vacation certificates, 562 or 78.1 percent were children of native born American fathers, 514 were white and 48 colored. The Italian group was the next largest with 6.8 percent. The Polish group accounted for 6.4 percent.

Following this report are the tables that indicate in further detail the distribution of these children according to industry and occupation entered, certificates issued, age, color, and sex.

## Counties of Maryland

The Maryland law provides that employment certificates outside of Baltimore City be issued by the Commissioner of Labor and Statistics, by the Superintendent of Schools in the county in which the applicant resides, or by some person designated in writing by the Superintendent. Since the issuing of these certificates entailed too much extra work for busy school officials, who received no remuneration for the work, it was agreed in 1914 by all interested parties that this responsibility could most logically be placed in the hands of the examining physicians who received compensation, although very meager at that time. Another consideration that prompted the change was the fact that the physician is constantly at his post, while the school officials are frequently away from the community during the canning season when the demand for certificates is greatest.

There is no part of the child labor law that requires greater accuracy and discrimination than the issuance of certificates. Experience in issuing certificates has shown conclusively that serious concentration upon the details of the law is a necessity. The examining physicians are busy men; they have not as much time to master the details of certificate issuance as have the regularly appointed city officials. There is no appropriation for personal supervision from the Baltimore office, therefore, supervision is carried on by correspondence, which has proved to be a very poor substitute. Consequently, the issuance of employment certificates in the counties is not as accurate as is desirable. During the coming year this recently re-organized division will concentrate on this problem to see if it is possible to work out some better method.

*Employment Certificates Issued:*

In 1936, 499 employment certificates were issued in the counties of Maryland, an increase of 116.9 percent over 1935. Of this number, 69 were first regular certificates, 428 first vacation certificates, and 2 were subsequent vacation certificates. These figures do not include the vocational or "special" certificates discussed elsewhere in the report, nor the 32 certificates which were revoked because it was found that the children involved did not meet the legal requirements.

Figures for Baltimore, Anne Arundel, and Howard Counties are included in the Baltimore City report, as these counties are considered part of the Baltimore Industrial Area.

*Revoked Certificates:*

It is provided that, for sufficient reason, a certificate may be revoked at any time and the dismissal of the child ordered. During the past year the division took over the verification of ages for all the children to whom certificates were issued in the counties. This has involved a tremendous amount of work, but has been found justifiable as a means of greater protection to our county children. Either through misinterpretation of the law or lack of familiarity with its requirements, many mistakes of serious nature were found in the issuance of county certificates, and involved the revocation of 32 certificates. Twenty-seven of this number were found to be under 14 years of age: 1 child proved to be only 11 years of age; 2 were 12 years of age; 24 were 13 years of age. Five children under 16 years of age were licensed to work in occupations forbidden under the law. Unfortunately, these errors do not come to the division until after the children involved have been working for some time, and it is this aspect of the situation that causes grave concern.

Next in order to the number of certificates issued illegally to children under age and for forbidden occupations is the number issued to children whose permanent residence is in Baltimore City. The canners employing children and the officers appointed to issue certificates to cover this employment have been notified that Baltimore children who migrate to the counties to work during the canning season must secure their certificates in Baltimore before leaving the city. This is necessary because of the difficulty of securing proper proof of age when the applicant for the certificate is away from his home. This procedure eliminates also an additional expense to the State during the children's temporary stay in the county as two salaried physicians are employed by this Department to examine all Baltimore City applicants.

## Statements of Age

During 1936 in Baltimore City, 1,493 children, 788 boys and 705 girls, gave satisfactory proof that they were over 16 years of age and were given statements to that effect by this division. Sixty-six of the 1,493 statements issued were subsequent statements. This is indicative of the care that a large number of employers exercise in order to prevent violation of the child labor law.

In the various counties of Maryland in 1936, 213 children, 78 boys and 135 girls, secured statements of age. Age statements which may be issued only to children 16 years of age or over had been issued to 9 children under 16 years. These statements were revoked during the year, and are not included in the above figure.

## School Attendance Department

There is the closest cooperation between the Baltimore City School Attendance Department and the Children's Division. Names and addresses of all refused applicants are sent each day to the Attendance Department. These reports are followed up by the attendance officers and their findings are reported back to this division. The Attendance Department in turn makes inquiry of this division every few days to learn if children who have left school and are reported to be at work have actually secured employment certificates. By this system of double reporting, a child who is known to either this division or to the Attendance Department cannot very easily violate either the child labor or compulsory school attendance law.

We are happy to state that during the past three months we have been able to establish a closer working relationship with the attendance deparments in the various counties. The county attendance officers are receiving from this office a list of all children to whom certificates of any kind have been issued by the examining physicians. If the attendance officers discover any discrepancies in the ages given, they notify this division immediately.

## Violations

Violations come to the attention of the Department principally through two sources—by the officials issuing employment certificates or by the industrial inspectors. During 1936 the industrial inspectors in Baltimore City reported violations of the child labor law in 122 establishments involving the illegal employment of 144 children; 78 involved the employment of children between the ages of 14 and 16 years without employment certificates; 37 were engaged in forbidden occupations; 18 children were under 14 years of age; 11 were working more than 8 hours a day or after 7 P. M. The repeal of prohibition and the return to the manufacture and sale of alcoholic liquors and beverages have brought additional problems connected with child labor and the need for enforcing the appropriate legal age provisions.

The Children's Division follows up all violations discovered by the inspectors and cooperates with the Chief Inspector by checking all records of possible suspects brought into the office by the inspectors. This involves a great amount of work, as it is often necessary to write to several sources before the child's correct age can be ascertained.

The policy of the Department during the past year has been to educate the community through a careful administration of the Child Labor Law rather than to prosecute violators. Only one employer was prosecuted in 1936. This employer, after warning and careful instructions from the department, violated the law a second time. A conviction was secured, the fine imposed was $10.00 and costs.

The above violations, all reported by the industrial inspectors, do not include 166 additional children who were employed in violation of the law and became known when they applied for employment certificates. Some were reported through the School Attendance Department. The number of children illegally employed, totaled 310.

In the counties of Maryland during 1936, violations of the child labor law were reported in 45 establishments involving the illegal employment of 90 children. This figure does not include the 32 county certificates that it was found necessary to revoke. Of the 90 children, 42 between the ages of 14 and 16 years, were found working without employment certificates; 25 children were under the minimum age for employment; and 23 were engaged in forbidden occupations. Of the 25 children working under 14 years of age, 1 was 10 years of age; 2 were 11 years of age; 8 were 12 years of age; and 14 were 13 years of age. Violations were cleared through correspondence. through the assistance of our inspector assigned to the Eastern Shore, and through the cooperation of the county attendance officers.


In addition to the children who received certificates to work, the Attendance Department of Baltimore City reported a total number of 568 children under 16 years who were permanently withdrawn from school for domestic service.

Figures secured through the State Industrial Accident Commission reveal the startling fact that 1,377 minors between the ages of 11 and 21 years met with accidents during the period from November 1, 1935 to November 1, 1936.

## NUMBER OF REGULAR, VACATION, AND VOCATIONAL CERTIFICATES SECURED BY CHILDREN IN BALTIMORE CITY IN 1936

| Kind of Certificate | Total Number | Regular | | | Vacation | | | Vocational | | |
|---|---|---|---|---|---|---|---|---|---|---|
| | | Total Number | Boys | Girls | Total Number | Boys | Girls | Total Number | Boys | Girls |
| Total number ...... | 1,455 | 399 | 347 | 52 | 386 | 336 | 50 | 670 | 424 | 246 |
| First.............. | 923 | 355 | 305 | 50 | 365 | 315 | 50 | 203 | 139 | 64 |
| Subsequent....... | 532 | 44 | 42 | 2 | 21 | 21 | ... | 467* | 285 | 182 |

*Includes both subsequent certificates and renewals. (See report of Special Permit Department for further information.)

EVIDENCE OF AGE SUBMITTED BY CHILDREN (14-16 YEARS) SECURING FIRST REGULAR AND VACATION
EMPLOYMENT CERTIFICATES IN BALTIMORE CITY IN 1936

| Evidence of Age Submitted | Total Number | Percent | Kind of Certificate | |
|---|---|---|---|---|
| | | | Regular | Vacation |
| Total number ........................ | 720 | 100.0 | 355 | 365 |
| Baltimore birth record.............. | 438 | 60.8 | 214 | 224 |
| Maryland birth record.............. | 39 | 5.4 | 20 | 19 |
| Other State birth record........... | 28 | 3.9 | 11 | 17 |
| Religious record ................... | 173 | 24.0 | 90 | 83 |
| Passport ........................... | 9 | 1.3 | 3 | 6 |
| Affidavit and physical examination... | 33 | 4.6 | 17 | 16 |

NUMBER OF CHILDREN (14-16 YEARS) SECURING FIRST REGULAR EMPLOYMENT CERTIFICATES IN BALTIMORE CITY IN 1936, BY LAST GRADE COMPLETED, AGE, COLOR, AND SEX

| Last Grade Completed | Total Number | Boys | | | | | Girls | | | | |
|---|---|---|---|---|---|---|---|---|---|---|---|
| | | Total Number | White | | Colored | | Total Number | White | | Colored | |
| | | | 14 | 15 | 14 | 15 | | 14 | 15 | 14 | 15 |
| Total number | 355 | 305 | 58 | 229 | 7 | 11 | 50 | 14 | 36 | ... | ... |
| Sixth | 121 | 110 | 20 | 84 | 4 | 2 | 11 | 4 | 7 | ... | ... |
| Seventh | 113 | 101 | 25 | 69 | 2 | 5 | 12 | 4 | 8 | ... | ... |
| Eighth | 77 | 58 | 8 | 45 | 1 | 4 | 19 | 5 | 14 | ... | ... |
| Ninth | 34 | 30 | 4 | 26 | ... | ... | 4 | ... | 4 | ... | ... |
| Tenth | 10 | 6 | 1 | 5 | ... | ... | 4 | 1 | 3 | ... | ... |

NUMBER OF CHILDREN (14-16 YEARS) SECURING FIRST REGULAR EMPLOYMENT CERTIFICATES IN BALTIMORE CITY IN 1936, BY OCCUPATION AND INDUSTRY ENTERED, AGE, COLOR, AND SEX

| Occupation and Industry Entered | Total Number | Percent | Boys | | | | | Girls | | | | |
|---|---|---|---|---|---|---|---|---|---|---|---|---|
| | | | Total Number | White 14 | White 15 | Colored 14 | Colored 15 | Total Number | White 14 | White 15 | Colored 14 | Colored 15 |
| Total number | 355 | 100.0 | 305 | 58 | 229 | 7 | 11 | 50 | 14 | 36 | .. | .. |
| Manufacturing and mechanical | 119 | 33.5 | 91 | 21 | 68 | 1 | 1 | 28 | 5 | 23 | .. | .. |
| Canning | 11 | 9.2 | 6 | 2 | 4 | .. | .. | 5 | 1 | 4 | .. | .. |
| Apprentices | 16 | 13.5 | 15 | 4 | 11 | .. | .. | 1 | 1 | .. | .. | .. |
| Operatives | 15 | 12.6 | 8 | 3 | 5 | .. | .. | 7 | 1 | 6 | .. | .. |
| Other manufacturing and mechanical | 77 | 64.7 | 62 | 12 | 48 | 1 | 1 | 15 | 2 | 13 | .. | .. |
| Mercantile | 96 | 27.1 | 81 | 12 | 67 | .. | 2 | 15 | 6 | 9 | .. | .. |
| Selling | 43 | 44.8 | 35 | 6 | 29 | .. | .. | 8 | 2 | 6 | .. | .. |
| Cash, bundle, messenger | 14 | 14.6 | 13 | 1 | 11 | .. | 1 | 1 | .. | 1 | .. | .. |
| Other mercantile | 39 | 40.6 | 33 | 5 | 27 | .. | 1 | 6 | 4 | 2 | .. | .. |
| Other occupation groups | 140 | 39.4 | 133 | 25 | 94 | 6 | 8 | 7 | 3 | 4 | .. | .. |
| Office work | 22 | 15.7 | 20 | 5 | 15 | .. | .. | 2 | 1 | 1 | .. | .. |
| Outside messenger or delivery | 83 | 59.3 | 83 | 15 | 61 | 4 | 3 | .. | .. | .. | .. | .. |
| Domestic and personal service | 17 | 12.2 | 12 | .. | 6 | 2 | 4 | 5 | 2 | 3 | .. | .. |
| Caddies | 16 | 11.4 | 16 | 5 | 11 | .. | .. | .. | .. | .. | .. | .. |
| Other | 2 | 1.4 | 2 | .. | 1 | .. | 1 | .. | .. | .. | .. | .. |

TIMORE CITY IN 1936, BY OCCUPATION AND INDUSTRY ENTERED, AGE, COLOR, AND SEX

| Occupation and Industry Entered | Total | | Boys | | | | | Girls | | | | |
|---|---|---|---|---|---|---|---|---|---|---|---|---|
| | | | | White | | Colored | | | White | | Colored | |
| | Number | Percent | Total Number | 14 | 15 | 14 | 15 | Total Number | 14 | 15 | 14 | 15 |
| Total number | 365 | 100.0 | 315 | 168 | 117 | 16 | 14 | 50 | 23 | 27 | ... | ... |
| Manufacturing and mechanical | 96 | 26.3 | 62 | 29 | 29 | 3 | 1 | 34 | 11 | 23 | ... | ... |
| Canning | 48 | 50.0 | 27 | 13 | 12 | 1 | 1 | 21 | 9 | 12 | ... | ... |
| Apprentices | 3 | 3.1 | 3 | 3 | ... | ... | ... | ... | ... | ... | ... | ... |
| Operatives | 14 | 14.6 | 6 | 3 | 3 | ... | ... | 8 | 2 | 6 | ... | ... |
| Other manufacturing and mechanical | 31 | 32.3 | 26 | 10 | 14 | 2 | ... | 5 | ... | 5 | ... | ... |
| Mercantile | 66 | 18.1 | 55 | 21 | 23 | 9 | 2 | 11 | 7 | 4 | ... | ... |
| Selling | 37 | 56.0 | 27 | 11 | 12 | 3 | 1 | 10 | 7 | 3 | ... | ... |
| Cash, bundle, messenger | 5 | 7.6 | 5 | ... | 3 | 1 | 1 | ... | ... | ... | ... | ... |
| Other mercantile | 24 | 36.4 | 23 | 10 | 8 | 5 | ... | 1 | ... | 1 | ... | ... |
| Other occupation groups | 203 | 55.6 | 198 | 118 | 65 | 4 | 11 | 5 | 5 | ... | ... | ... |
| Office work | 8 | 3.9 | 5 | 2 | 3 | ... | ... | 3 | 3 | ... | ... | ... |
| Outside messenger or delivery | 71 | 35.0 | 71 | 38 | 26 | 1 | 6 | ... | ... | ... | ... | ... |
| Domestic and personal service | 10 | 4.9 | 9 | 3 | 1 | 1 | 4 | 1 | 1 | ... | ... | ... |
| Caddies | 110 | 54.2 | 110 | 75 | 35 | ... | ... | ... | ... | ... | ... | ... |
| Other | 4 | 2.0 | 3 | ... | ... | 2 | 1 | 1 | 1 | ... | ... | ... |

NUMBER OF FIRST EMPLOYMENT CERTIFICATES ISSUED IN BALTIMORE CITY BY MONTH, SEX, AND KIND OF CERTIFICATE: 1936 AND 1935

| Month and Year | Total Number | Kind of Certificate | | | |
|---|---|---|---|---|---|
| | | Regular | | Vacation | |
| | | Boys | Girls | Boys | Girls |
| Baltimore City..1936 | 720 | 305 | 50 | 315 | 50 |
| 1935 | 457 | 126 | 22 | 289 | 20 |
| January .....1936 | 23 | 16 | 2 | 5 | .. |
| 1935 | 2 | .. | .. | 2 | .. |
| February ....1936 | 24 | 15 | 5 | 4 | .. |
| 1935 | 6 | .. | .. | 6 | .. |
| March .......1936 | 43 | 27 | 2 | 13 | 1 |
| 1935 | 3 | 1 | .. | 2 | .. |
| April ........1936 | 56 | 33 | 3 | 20 | .. |
| 1935 | 13 | .. | .. | 10 | 3 |
| May .........1936 | 80 | 43 | 4 | 32 | 1 |
| 1935 | 13 | 2 | .. | 11 | .. |
| June ........1936 | 115 | 16 | 3 | 86 | 10 |
| 1935 | 37 | 5 | 2 | 27 | 3 |
| July ........1936 | 101 | 4 | 1 | 78 | 18 |
| 1935 | 147 | .. | 1 | 144 | 2 |
| August ......1936 | 59 | 2 | .. | 39 | 18 |
| 1935 | 61 | .. | 1 | 50 | 10 |
| September ...1936 | 78 | 64 | 10 | 4 | .. |
| 1935 | 54 | 30 | 6 | 18 | .. |
| October .....1936 | 72 | 39 | 12 | 19 | 2 |
| 1935 | 62 | 53 | 7 | 2 | .. |
| November ...1936 | 43 | 30 | 4 | 9 | .. |
| 1935 | 34 | 21 | 3 | 9 | 1 |
| December ...1936 | 26 | 16 | 4 | 6 | .. |
| 1935 | 25 | 14 | 2 | 8 | 1 |

NUMBER OF REGULAR AND VACATION EMPLOYMENT CERTIFICATES
SECURED BY CHILDREN IN THE COUNTIES IN 1936

| Kind of Certificate | Total Number | Regular | | | Vacation | | |
|---|---|---|---|---|---|---|---|
| | | Total Number | Boys | Girls | Total Number | Boys | Girls |
| Total number | 499 | 69 | 37 | 32 | 430 | 224 | 206 |
| First | 497 | 69 | 37 | 32 | 428 | 223 | 205 |
| Subsequent | 2 | .. | .. | .. | 2 | 1 | 1 |

NUMBER OF CHILDREN (14-16 YEARS) SECURING EMPLOYMENT CERTIFICATES IN THE COUNTIES IN 1936, BY OCCUPATION AND INDUSTRY ENTERED, SEX, AND KIND OF CERTIFICATE

| Occupation and Industry Entered | Total Number | Kind of Certificate | | | | | |
|---|---|---|---|---|---|---|---|
| | | Regular | | | Vacation | | |
| | | Total Number | Boys | Girls | Total Number | Boys | Girls |
| Total Number | 497 | 69 | 37 | 32 | 428 | 223 | 205 |
| Manufacturing and mechanical | 399 | 43 | 17 | 26 | 356 | 166 | 190 |
| Canning | 356 | 22 | 6 | 16 | 334 | 151 | 183 |
| Apprentices | 1 | ... | ... | ... | 1 | 1 | ... |
| Operatives | 12 | 6 | 1 | 5 | 6 | 1 | 5 |
| Other manufacturing and mechanical | 30 | 15 | 10 | 5 | 15 | 13 | 2 |
| Mercantile | 33 | 12 | 9 | 3 | 21 | 11 | 10 |
| Selling | 19 | 5 | 2 | 3 | 14 | 5 | 9 |
| Other mercantile | 14 | 7 | 7 | ... | 7 | 6 | 1 |
| Other occupation groups | 65 | 14 | 11 | 3 | 51 | 46 | 5 |
| Office work | 2 | 2 | 1 | 1 | ... | ... | ... |
| Outside messenger or delivery | 40 | 9 | 9 | ... | 31 | 31 | ... |
| Domestic and personal service | 15 | 3 | 1 | 2 | 12 | 8 | 4 |
| Caddies | 4 | ... | ... | ... | 4 | 4 | ... |
| Other | 4 | ... | ... | ... | 4 | 3 | 1 |

NUMBER OF CHILDREN (14-16 YEARS) SECURING FIRST EMPLOYMENT CERTIFICATES IN THE COUNTIES IN 1936, BY COUNTY, SEX, AND KIND OF CERTIFICATE

| County | Total Number | Kind of Certificate | | | | | |
|---|---|---|---|---|---|---|---|
| | | Regular | | | Vacation | | |
| | | Total Number | Boys | Girls | Total Number | Boys | Girls |
| Total number | 497 | 69 | 37 | 32 | 428 | 223 | 205 |
| Allegany | 5 | 4 | 4 | | 1 | 1 | |
| Caroline | 90 | 5 | 2 | 3 | 85 | 29 | 56 |
| Carroll | 46 | 10 | 3 | 7 | 36 | 19 | 17 |
| Cecil | 21 | | | | 21 | 17 | 4 |
| Dorchester | 84 | 8 | 7 | 1 | 76 | 33 | 43 |
| Frederick | 45 | 11 | 7 | 4 | 34 | 27 | 7 |
| Garrett | 2 | | | | 2 | 1 | 1 |
| Harford | 12 | | | | 12 | 6 | 6 |
| Kent | 5 | | | | 5 | 2 | 3 |
| Montgomery | 8 | 5 | 3 | 2 | 3 | 2 | 1 |
| Prince George's | 9 | 4 | 4 | | 5 | 5 | |
| Queen Anne's | 1 | 1 | | 1 | | | |
| Somerset | 26 | | | | 26 | 14 | 12 |
| Talbot | 70 | 3 | 1 | 2 | 67 | 35 | 32 |
| Washington | 5 | | | | 5 | 5 | |
| Wicomico | 44 | 12 | 4 | 8 | 32 | 19 | 13 |
| Worcester | 24 | 6 | 2 | 4 | 18 | 8 | 10 |

## Special Employment Certificates

One of the functions of the office of the Commissioner of Labor and Statistics is to carry out the provisions of an Act passed by the General Assembly of Marylnd in 1918 relating to "backward school children." The purpose of this Act was to render assistance to the mentally handicapped children of working age who naturally would have difficulty in securing employment and in becoming self-supporting and law-abiding citizens. Under proper supervision many of these unfortunate children are able to make satisfactory vocational adjustments and become social assets rather than liabilities.

None of the children is released from school until a complete study of the applicant has been made and until a conference has been held on each child with the proper school officials, the Director of Special Education in the Baltimore Department of Public Education, or the Superintendent of Education in the Parochial Schools. If it is felt that the child may benefit from further schooling by being transferred to another type of school or class, this is tried before the final release from school is approved.

In 1936, 374 children between the ages of 14 and 16 years applied to this division for first special work permits, an increase of 148, or 65.5 percent, over the number of applicants applying in 1935. This condition was due partly to the termination of the restrictions placed on child labor by the NRA and to the increase in employment opportunities. Two hundred seventy-two of these children were referred by City and County Departments of education, by social agencies, and by mental hygiene clinics. Two hundred three of these children received permits and 69 were refused and returned to school, as it was felt that these children could profit by further schooling. Some were returned because they had physical defects which needed attention and follow-up from the school nursing service. The remaining 102 were neither referred by the departments of education nor social agencies, but made personal application to the office. As this group did not have the necessary educational sheets approved by the principals of the schools, they were referred to the Director of School Attendance for further investigation.

Of the 272 children mentioned above, 29 were referred from the counties of Maryland as follows: Baltimore County, 22; Anne Arundel, 2; Dorchester, 1; Howard, 2; St. Mary's, 1; Talbot, 1.

After a child has been released from school on a special permit he must report to this office at the end of every two months until ie reaches tie age of sixteen. If ie 1as made satisfactory progress by tiat time and appears to be a stable individual witi good ciaracter traits, ie tien reports every four montis until ie is eigiteen years of age.

Tie individuals in boti groups are instructed to report immediately, iowever, if tie jobs on wiici tiey are employed terminate for any reason. On tie ciild's return visit to tie office ie is interviewed, iis piysical condition ciecked, and, if ie 1as tie same job, iis permit is renewed. In addition to tie original permits issued in 1936, 427 renewals were issued to ciildren under sixteen years of age, 250 to boys and 177 to girls. If tie ciild 1as secured a new job ie is given a "subsequent" permit. Forty subsequent permits were issued for ciildren under sixteen years of age, 35 to boys and 5 to girls. During tie year 373 individuals between tie ages of sixteen and eigiteen reported to tiis office and renewals and subsequents were issued to tiem in tie same manner.

As usual, by far tie largest group who secured first special permits in Baltimore City during 1936 1ad been born in Baltimore City. While 79.0 percent were in tiis group, tie next largest number, 8.9 percent, had been born in otier States.

As evidence of age, 78.3 percent of all first special permits were issued upon receipt of official birti records and 18.4 percent upon baptismal certificates. In otier words, 96.7 percent of all first permits were issued upon some documentary evidence of age. Only 3.3 percent were issued upon tie affidavit of parents.

During tie year tie workers in tie special employment certificate division held over 1,828 interviews. Tiis figure does not include visits to tie 1omes, sciools, and social agencies.

## VOCATIONAL

| Kind of Certificate | Total | Boys | Girls |
|---|---|---|---|
| Total number (including home and domestic service permits).. | 670 | 424 | 246 |
| First ..................... | 203 | 139 | 64 |
| Subsequents* ... ........... | 467 | 285 | 182 |

*Includes both subsequent certificates and renewals.

NUMBER OF CHILDREN REFERRED FOR SPECIAL EMPLOY-
MENT CERTIFICATES BY CITY AND COUNTY DEPARTMENTS
OF EDUCATION IN 1936

| Month | Total Number | Permits Granted | | Withdrawn for Domestic Service | | Returned to School | |
|---|---|---|---|---|---|---|---|
| | | Male | Female | Male | Female | Male | Female |
| Total number .... | 272 | 126 | 12 | 13 | 52 | 46 | 23 |
| January ....... | 24 | 11 | 1 | .. | 6 | 3 | 3 |
| February ...... | 22 | 9 | .. | .. | 6 | 3 | 4 |
| March ......... | 24 | 4 | 3 | 6 | 4 | 4 | 3 |
| April ......... | 19 | 7 | 3 | 3 | 2 | 2 | 2 |
| May .......... | 28 | 11 | .. | 1 | 6 | 8 | 2 |
| June ......... | 20 | 10 | .. | .. | 6 | 4 | .. |
| July........... | .. | .. | .. | .. | .. | .. | .. |
| August ....... | 4 | 3 | 1 | .. | .. | .. | .. |
| September .... | 39 | 24 | 3 | 1 | 3 | 5 | 3 |
| October....... | 44 | 22 | 1 | .. | 12 | 6 | 3 |
| November ..... | 33 | 21 | .. | 1 | 5 | 5 | 1 |
| December ..... | 15 | 4 | .. | 1 | 2 | 6 | 2 |

EVIDENCE OF AGE SUBMITTED BY CHILDREN (14-16 YEARS)
REFERRED FOR SPECIAL EMPLOYMENT CERTIFICATES IN 1936

| Evidence of Age Submitted | Total Number | Per-cent |
|---|---|---|
| Total number ......................................... | 272 | 100.0 |
| Baltimore birth record............................. | 177 | 65.1 |
| Maryland birth record.............................. | 24 | 8.8 |
| Other State birth record............................ | 11 | 4.0 |
| Religious certificates .............................. | 50 | 18.4 |
| Affidavit ......................................... | 9 | 3.3 |
| Foreign ... .......................................... | 1 | .4 |

## Report of Medical Examiners

During the year 1936 the Medical Examiners made a total of 1,025 first examinations and 170 re-examinations of applicants for employment certificates. There were also a number of physical examinations of newsboys made for verification of age.

Of the total number of first examinations, 821 were boys and 204 were girls, and 622 children were found to have one or more physical defects. During 1935 only 14 cases reported correction of physical defects, while in 1936 in the regular and vacation employment certificate group 31 reported correction of physical defects. Many corrections were noted in the special employment certificate group.

It is very apparent that with the increase of industrial activity the parents of these children are in a better financial position to attend to the physical ailments found in their children, and, in many cases whenever possible, to have these conditions corrected. This is especially true of those children with defective vision and carious teeth, as well as a number of children who have had diseased tonsils removed.

Just as we have noted in the past few years, the most common outstanding physical defect was under-weight; 270 children being under-weight in the year 1936 as compared with 151 in the year 1935. In the order of their frequency the next most common defective conditions noted were as follows: carious teeth, 231; defective vision, 132; enlarged cryptic tonsils, 76; over-weight, 51. One hundred seventy-two children had 2 physical defects, 31 had 3 physical defects, and 2 had 4 physical defects.

Among the least common defective physical conditions noted were: disease of the thyroid gland; heart disease; complete nasal obstruction, in some cases producing a speech defect; pregnancy; suspected tuberculosis; deafness; gonorrhea; and hernia.

## Newsboys and Street-Traders

In compliance with the legal provisions for the licensing of newsboys and street-traders, there are five distinct types of badges issued in Maryland: (1) a route service badge, which permits a boy of ten years or more to serve papers around a regular route between certain specified hours of the day; (2) an oval newsboy badge, which permits a boy of twelve years or more to sell papers on the street during certain hours when school is not in session; (3) a square newsboy badge, which permits a boy of fourteen or fifteen years of age to sell papers at any time between the hours of six o'clock in the morning and eight o'clock in the evening; (4) an oval street-trader badge which permits a boy of fourteen years or more to sell articles other than papers on the street during certain hours when school is not in session; (5) a square street-trader badge, which permits a boy of fourteen or fifteen years of age to sell articles other than papers on the street at any time between the hours of six o'clock in the morning and eight o'clock in the evening. These badges are issued in cities having a population of 20,000 persons or over.

In 1936 this division issued 2,163 licenses in Baltimore, 208 in Cumberland, and 125 in Hagerstown and refused 22 licenses in Baltimore, 6 licenses in Cumberland, and 8 licenses in Hagerstown. The number of badges returned in Maryland was 481. These were returned by boys who had attained the age after which a badge is no longer required. In many cases they requested statements proving their age was 16 years or over in order to procure other employment. Ten theatre permits were issued permitting the children involved to appear on a public stage for a limited time.

Violations of the newsboy law were reported for 1,197 cases and included 7 girls and 11 agents. These violations were dealt with directly by this division and, where necessary, were sent to the Juvenile Court for further consideration. As a result of violations of the law the badges of 22 boys were revoked for varying periods of time.

The following tables give in detail the distribution of newsboy and street-trader licenses, theatre permits, and violations of the newsboy law.

NUMBER OF NEWSBOY AND STREET-TRADER LICENSES ISSUED
IN BALTIMORE CITY, CUMBERLAND, AND HAGERSTOWN IN
1936, BY KIND OF LICENSE AND COLOR

## Baltimore City

| Kind of License | Total number | First | | Renewed | |
|---|---|---|---|---|---|
| | | White | Colored | White | Colored |
| Total number ....... | 2,163 | 965 | 180 | 770 | 248 |
| Route service ..... | 56 | 39 | 10 | 6 | 1 |
| Oval newsboy .... | 1,900 | 776 | 147 | 735 | 242 |
| Square newsboy... | 94* | 78 | 6 | 8 | 2 |
| Oval street-trader. | 69 | 38 | 15 | 13 | 3 |
| Square street-trader | 44† | 34 | 2 | 8 | .. |

*Includes 10 vocational in Baltimore City.
†Includes 14 vocational in Baltimore City.

## Cumberland

| Kind of License | Total number | First | | Renewed | |
|---|---|---|---|---|---|
| | | White | Colored | White | Colored |
| Total number ....... | 208 | 107 | .. | 99 | 2 |
| Route service ..... | 23 | 20 | .. | 3 | .. |
| Oval newsboy .... | 185 | 87 | .. | 96 | 2 |
| Square newsboy... | .. | .. | .. | .. | .. |
| Oval street-trader. | .. | .. | .. | .. | .. |
| Square street-trader | .. | .. | .. | .. | .. |

## Hagerstown

| Kind of License | Total number | First | | Renewed | |
|---|---|---|---|---|---|
| | | White | Colored | White | Colored |
| Total number ....... | 125 | 72 | .. | 52 | 1 |
| Route service ..... | 7 | 7 | .. | .. | .. |
| Oval newsboy .... | 118 | 65 | .. | 52 | 1 |
| Square newsboy... | .. | .. | .. | .. | .. |
| Oval street-trader. | .. | .. | .. | .. | .. |
| Square street-trader | .. | .. | .. | .. | .. |

NUMBER OF BOYS REFUSED LICENSES IN BALTIMORE CITY IN
1936, BY AGE AND KIND OF LICENSE

| Age in Years | Total Number | Route Service | Oval Newsboy | Oval Street-trader |
|---|---|---|---|---|
| Total number ......... | 22 | 4 | 12 | 6 |
| 10 years ........... | 7 | 3 | 4 | .. |
| 11 years ........... | 10 | 1 | 8 | 1 |
| 12 years ........... | 3 | .. | .. | 3 |
| 13 years ........... | 2 | .. | .. | 2 |

NUMBER OF FIRST NEWSBOY AND STREET-TRADER LICENSES
ISSUED IN BALTIMORE CITY IN 1936, BY AGE AND
KIND OF LICENSE

| Age | Total Number | First Route Service | First Oval Newsboy | First Square Newsboy | First Oval Street-Trader | First Square St. Trader |
|---|---|---|---|---|---|---|
| Total number ......... | 1,145 | 49 | 923 | 84 | 53 | 36 |
| 10 years ........... | 11 | 11 | .. | .. | .. | .. |
| 11 years ........... | 38 | 38 | .. | .. | .. | .. |
| 12 years ........... | 422 | .. | 422 | .. | .. | .. |
| 13 years ........... | 252 | .. | 252 | .. | .. | .. |
| 14 years ........... | 250 | .. | 179 | 19 | 39 | 13 |
| 15 years ........... | 172 | .. | 70 | 65 | 14 | 23 |

NUMBER OF FIRST NEWSBOY AND STREET-TRADER LICENSES
ISSUED IN MARYLAND IN 1936, BY EVIDENCE OF AGE

| Evidence of Age | Total Number | Percent | Baltimore | Cumberland | Hagerstown |
|---|---|---|---|---|---|
| Total number ..................... | 1,324 | 100.0 | 1,145 | 107 | 72 |
| Baltimore birth record............ | 922 | 69.6 | 921 | ... | 1 |
| Maryland birth record............ | 191 | 14.4 | 52 | 82 | 57 |
| Other State birth record.......... | 100 | 7.6 | 77 | 16 | 7 |
| Foreign birth record.............. | 3 | 0.2 | 3 | ... | ... |
| Religious certificate .............. | 79 | 6.0 | 66 | 7 | 6 |
| Other document ................. | 3 | 0.2 | 3 | ... | ... |
| Affidavit and physical examination................................... | 26 | 2.0 | 23 | 2 | 1 |

NUMBER OF NEWSBOY AND STREET-TRADER VIOLATIONS
REPORTED IN BALTIMORE CITY IN 1936

| Source of Report | Number of Violations |
|---|---|
| Total number .............................. | 1,197* |
| By Inspectors ............................. | 1,168 |
| By Police Department....................... | 1 |
| By School Attendance Department........... | 15 |
| By other sources........................... | 13 |

*Includes 11 agents or dealers and 7 girls.

NUMBER OF CHILDREN AND AGENTS TAKEN TO JUVENILE
COURT IN BALTIMORE CITY IN 1936, BY NATURE OF VIOLA-
TION

| Nature of Violation | Number of Children and Agents | | | |
|---|---|---|---|---|
| | Total Number | Boys | Girls | Agents |
| Total number ................... | 91 | 84 | 3 | 4 |
| Bootblack...................... | 4 | 4 | .. | .. |
| Disorderly conduct ............. | 2 | 2 | .. | .. |
| Furnished bags to unlicensed boys. ...................... | 1 | .. | .. | 1 |
| Furnished magazines and papers to unlicensed boys............ | 3 | .. | .. | 3 |
| Selling bags, no badge.......... | 44 | 42 | 2 | .. |
| Selling candy, no badge......... | 1 | .. | 1 | .. |
| Selling flowers, no badge........ | 1 | 1 | .. | .. |
| Selling magazines, no badge..... | 4 | 4 | .. | .. |
| Selling papers, no badge........ | 23 | 23 | .. | .. |
| Selling, prohibited hours........ | 7 | 7 | .. | .. |
| Selling shoestrings, no badge.... | 1 | 1 | .. | .. |

NUMBER OF CHILDREN AND AGENTS TAKEN TO JUVENILE
COURT IN BALTIMORE CITY IN 1936, BY DISPOSITION OF
CASE

| Disposition of Case | Number of Children and Agents | | | |
| --- | --- | --- | --- | --- |
| | Total Number | Boys | Girls | Agents |
| Total number ................... | 91 | 84 | 3 | 4 |
| Committed to care of Hebrew Children Society ............. | 1 | 1 | .. | .. |
| Committed to St. Mary's Industrial School .................. | 1 | 1 | .. | .. |
| Dismissed with warning......... | 5 | 2 | .. | 3 |
| Fined $6.45 ................... | 1 | .. | .. | 1 |
| Informal probation ............. | 71 | 71 | .. | .. |
| On probation ................. | 12 | 9 | 3 | .. |

NUMBER OF UNLICENSED CHILDREN SUMMONED TO BALTI-
MORE OFFICE IN 1936

| Nature of Violation | Number of Children Summoned | | |
| --- | --- | --- | --- |
| | Total Number | Boys | Girls |
| Total number .......................... | 296* | 292 | 4 |
| Bootblack .... ......................... | 7 | 7 | .. |
| Distributing circulars .................. | 3 | 3 | .. |
| Selling bags ......................... | 44 | 43 | 1 |
| Selling candy ........................ | 7 | 5 | 2 |
| Selling flowers ....................... | 7 | 6 | 1 |
| Selling fruit ......................... | 6 | 6 | .. |
| Selling magazines ..................... | 36 | 36 | .. |
| Selling papers ........................ | 182 | 182 | .. |
| Selling peanuts ....................... | 2 | 2 | .. |
| Selling produce....................... | 1 | 1 | .. |
| Selling shoestrings ................... | 1 | 1 | .. |

*Seven agents were also summoned and warned.

NUMBER OF BOYS HAVING LICENSES SUMMONED TO
BALTIMORE OFFICE IN 1936

| Nature of Violation | Number of Boys |
|---|---|
| Total number | 48 |
| Badge, not worn | 32 |
| Had unlicensed boy selling | 1 |
| Selling after 8 P. M. | 9 |
| Selling during school hours | 2 |
| Selling on route service badge | 4 |

NUMBER OF PARENTS NOTIFIED OF VIOLATIONS BY LETTERS
FROM BALTIMORE OFFICE IN 1936

| Nature of Violation | Number of Parents Notified | | |
|---|---|---|---|
| | Total Number | Boys | Girls |
| Total number | 733 | 732 | 1 |
| Licensed boys | 86 | 86 | .. |
| Badge broken, not worn | 17 | 17 | .. |
| Badge lost | 3 | 3 | .. |
| Badge, not worn | 66 | 66 | .. |
| Unlicensed children | 647 | 646 | 1 |
| Distributing circulars | 34 | 34 | .. |
| Selling bags | 12 | 12 | .. |
| Selling flowers and candy | 6 | 5 | 1 |
| Selling magazines | 99 | 99 | .. |
| Selling papers | 491 | 491 | .. |
| Selling peanuts | 1 | 1 | .. |
| Selling produce | 4 | 4 | .. |

## NUMBER OF NEWSBOY AND STREET-TRADER LICENSES REVOKED IN BALTIMORE CITY IN 1936

| Nature of Violation | Total Number | Period of Time for which Revoked | | | | | | |
|---|---|---|---|---|---|---|---|---|
| | | 10 Days | 15 Days | 1 Month | 2 Months | 3 Months | 4 Months | 6 Months |
| Total number | 22 | 6 | 1 | 3 | 2 | 3 | 4 | 3 |
| Badge not worn | 1 | . | . | . | . | 1 | . | . |
| and badge to another | 2 | . | . | . | 1 | 1 | . | . |
| Had unlicensed boys selling | 4 | 1 | . | . | . | 1 | 1 | 1 |
| Misconduct in school | 3 | 1 | . | . | . | . | 2 | . |
| Selling after 8 P. M. | 5 | 3 | 1 | 1 | . | . | . | . |
| Selling during school hours | 3 | 1 | . | 1 | 1 | . | . | . |
| Selling on route badge | 2 | . | . | . | . | . | 1 | 1 |
| Truancy | 2 | . | . | 1 | . | . | . | 1 |

NUMBER OF CHILDREN SECURING PERMITS TO APPEAR IN THEATRES IN BALTIMORE CITY IN 1936, BY AGE, SEX, AND COLOR

| Age | Total Number | White | | | Colored | | |
|---|---|---|---|---|---|---|---|
| | | Total Number | Boys | Girls | Total Number | Boys | Girls |
| Total number. | 10 | 5 | 3 | 2 | 5 | 2 | 3 |
| 6 years .... | 1 | .. | .. | .. | 1 | 1 | .. |
| 7 years .... | 1 | .. | .. | .. | 1 | .. | 1 |
| 8 years .... | 1 | 1 | 1 | .. | .. | .. | .. |
| 9 years .... | 1 | .. | .. | .. | 1 | 1 | .. |
| 10 years .... | .. | .. | .. | .. | .. | .. | .. |
| 11 years .... | 3 | 2 | 2 | .. | 1 | .. | 1 |
| 12 years .... | 2 | 1 | .. | 1 | 1 | .. | 1 |
| 13 years .... | .. | .. | .. | .. | .. | .. | .. |
| 14 years .... | 1 | 1 | .. | 1 | .. | .. | .. |
| 15 years .... | .. | .. | .. | .. | .. | .. | .. |

## DIVISION OF STATISTICS

The past year has been the busiest this division has ever experienced. In addition to its regular work of maintaining statistical records of the department and conducting the regular monthly employment survey, this division has been called upon to furnish data in response to many and varied requests. In some instances when the information requested was not readily available the division has been unable to supply it because of limited personnel and funds. However, every effort is made to comply with requests for information and much valuable material was furnished which contributed to the success of many worthwhile projects and significantly aided the welfare of the people of the State.

It was the desire of this department, through the medium of a Works Progress Administration project, to make a survey of the wages, hours, and working conditions of employed women in Maryland. It was thought that data resulting from such a needed survey could be used to good advantage as a basis for more up-to-date legislation. It was with profound disappointment that this department learned that the federal agency that would ordinarily have sponsored such an undertaking was not sufficiently interested to approach the Works Progress Administration on this project.

Another study that would prove of interest to many Marylanders is a cost of living survey which this department is desirous of making but has been prevented from conducting because of insufficient personnel and lack of funds.

### Trends of Employment and Weekly Earnings

For a number of years this division has been compiling comparable statistical data showing the monthly trends of employment and weekly earnings in the various industries of the State.

There is a decided need for reliable statistics on this vital and important subject. That business and government need statistics to show the scope and extent of employment and earnings in the State as well as the extent of recovery under policies pursued, requires no positive argument. This division receives numerous requests for statistical data on the employment situation from the State Planning Commission, government agencies, relief organizations, business organizations, labor organizations, and interested citizens. For these reasons, the Commissioner of Labor and Statistics has endeavored to maintain a monthly survey of industry of concrete value to all. This office has been aided materially in this survey by unusually fine cooperation on the part of employers throughout the State.

The procedure used in compiling the monthly employment bulletin is as follows:

A report form is sent to each cooperating firm monthly with the request to fill in the following information: number of employees; amount of payroll; number of man-hours worked; and wage rate changes for the period reported. The forms are filled in according to usual pay periods which may be monthly, semi-monthly, bi-weekly, or weekly. Approximately 1,700 firms are canvassed monthly employing 125,000 persons with a $2,825,000 weekly payroll. All payrolls and man-hours are reduced to a weekly basis. From these data, tabulations are made for 43 manufacturing industries and 12 non-manufacturing industries and summaries for each industry are presented monthly in index number form, that is, as relatives stated in percentage of the selected base figure, the years 1929, 1930, and 1931.

Greater gains in employment and payrolls were recorded for the year 1936 than for any other year since the beginning of the depression late in 1929. This office is confident that these gains are of a permanent nature.

This department has been collecting statistics of this nature on employment and payrolls in the State since 1923. The extraordinary session of the General Assembly in 1936 passed a bill creating the Unemployment Compensation Administration, whose duty it will be to collect payroll data of a similar nature which will necessarily be a duplication of work in this field and a duplication of reports for employers. This department feels that the records and reports involved should be supervised from one department. It recommends that an arrangement be made that would relieve employers of duplication of reports and at the same time effect a real economy for the State of Maryland by providing a valuable opportunity for this office to expand in other statistical fields which would be of greater value to employer and employee interests.

The following tables show in detail the monthly trend of employment and weekly earnings in Maryland and Baltimore City:

## INDEX NUMBERS, EMPLOYMENT AND COMBINED WEEKLY PAYROLLS, STATE OF MARYLAND COMBINED MANUFACTURING INDUSTRIES

### (Average 36 months, 1929-1931 = 100.0)

Employment

| Months | 1924 | 1925 | 1926 | 1927 | 1928 | 1929 | 1930 | 1931 | 1932 | 1933 | 1934 | 1935 | 1936 |
|---|---|---|---|---|---|---|---|---|---|---|---|---|---|
| January | 131.3 | 122.7 | 127.6 | 122.2 | 108.4 | 105.1 | 103.5 | 87.8 | 77.1 | 65.3 | 79.0 | 84.9 | 88.4 |
| February | 129.0 | 125.1 | 128.0 | 124.0 | 111.9 | 107.7 | 105.7 | 90.2 | 77.4 | 67.3 | 83.8 | 87.9 | 88.3 |
| March | 126.8 | 129.3 | 129.2 | 123.9 | 113.8 | 111.0 | 106.3 | 91.8 | 77.7 | 64.2 | 86.7 | 89.3 | 90.5 |
| April | 129.3 | 128.2 | 127.3 | 123.7 | 112.3 | 111.8 | 107.3 | 93.1 | 76.9 | 67.4 | 90.3 | 90.7 | 93.1 |
| May | 126.2 | 122.4 | 126.0 | 120.9 | 111.2 | 112.1 | 106.3 | 92.9 | 72.5 | 68.2 | 89.4 | 89.5 | 94.2 |
| June | 123.4 | 123.1 | 124.9 | 120.0 | 109.5 | 111.5 | 104.9 | 88.7 | 68.1 | 71.0 | 87.6 | 88.2 | 93.9 |
| July | 121.1 | 123.1 | 123.8 | 117.3 | 107.1 | 111.0 | 100.4 | 87.9 | 65.9 | 78.8 | 87.0 | 86.5 | 95.5 |
| August | 118.3 | 124.4 | 124.4 | 119.2 | 108.5 | 111.9 | 99.8 | 87.8 | 66.4 | 83.8 | 86.2 | 88.8 | 98.2 |
| September | 122.1 | 127.7 | 128.1 | 119.3 | 110.4 | 113.2 | 102.4 | 87.6 | 68.9 | 88.3 | 86.7 | 92.3 | 98.9 |
| October | 126.3 | 128.3 | 127.5 | 116.2 | 112.2 | 112.0 | 100.2 | 84.8 | 70.9 | 90.1 | 85.4 | 92.1 | 100.2 |
| November | 124.1 | 125.7 | 125.0 | 110.7 | 108.9 | 110.3 | 94.1 | 81.2 | 69.8 | 85.5 | 85.5 | 90.4 | 99.5 |
| December | 123.9 | 128.3 | 124.3 | 111.3 | 108.4 | 107.6 | 91.2 | 80.5 | 69.3 | 81.2 | 85.5 | 89.7 | 99.1 |

Payrolls

## INDEX NUMBERS, EMPLOYMENT AND COMBINED WEEKLY PAYROLLS, BALTIMORE INDUSTRIAL AREA

### COMBINED MANUFACTURING INDUSTRIES

(Average 36 months, 1929-1931 = 100.0)

| Months | Employment | | | | | | | | Payrolls | | | | | | | |
|---|---|---|---|---|---|---|---|---|---|---|---|---|---|---|---|---|
| | 1929 | 1930 | 1931 | 1932 | 1933 | 1934 | 1935 | 1936 | 1929 | 1930 | 1931 | 1932 | 1933 | 1934 | 1935 | 1936 |
| January.. | 105.6 | 103.9 | 87.3 | 76.2 | 60.2 | 72.1 | 75.7 | 80.8 | 107.8 | 104.1 | 81.5 | 60.8 | 41.9 | 61.4 | 65.2 | 78.1 |
| February. | 108.3 | 106.3 | 89.7 | 76.4 | 62.5 | 76.1 | 78.4 | 82.0 | 118.1 | 111.8 | 87.1 | 60.0 | 42.0 | 65.9 | 72.0 | 80.3 |
| March.... | 112.1 | 107.5 | 91.2 | 76.6 | 59.5 | 79.6 | 80.2 | 83.3 | 121.7 | 114.8 | 87.1 | 59.8 | 40.9 | 70.6 | 76.1 | 80.9 |
| April..... | 113.2 | 109.2 | 92.6 | 76.6 | 63.4 | 84.6 | 83.3 | 86.2 | 122.2 | 114.7 | 88.3 | 58.4 | 43.2 | 75.3 | 78.5 | 85.4 |
| May....... | 112.8 | 107.4 | 91.9 | 72.5 | 62.7 | 84.5 | 82.6 | 87.7 | 121.1 | 111.5 | 86.1 | 53.4 | 45.7 | 76.6 | 77.0 | 91.3 |
| June....... | 112.0 | 105.3 | 87.3 | 69.0 | 64.0 | 81.9 | 80.8 | 88.2 | 119.8 | 107.1 | 80.6 | 50.5 | 49.3 | 77.6 | 76.4 | 92.9 |
| July....... | 111.7 | 100.5 | 86.5 | 65.0 | 70.0 | 81.6 | 79.4 | 88.9 | 116.9 | 100.1 | 76.2 | 46.1 | 55.6 | 75.4 | 73.9 | 92.7 |
| August.... | 112.4 | 100.2 | 86.5 | 64.5 | 75.5 | 80.1 | 80.9 | 91.1 | 117.4 | 99.7 | 79.4 | 45.6 | 63.2 | 68.8 | 77.1 | 95.2 |
| September | 114.9 | 102.2 | 86.8 | 65.7 | 79.1 | 80.6 | 84.5 | 91.5 | 117.9 | 103.1 | 76.6 | 46.8 | 68.8 | 68.9 | 81.6 | 96.9 |
| October... | 113.1 | 99.8 | 83.7 | 66.2 | 80.9 | 79.4 | 84.4 | 92.1 | 119.2 | 97.9 | 71.3 | 48.1 | 67.5 | 66.2 | 80.4 | 99.8 |
| November. | 111.9 | 93.4 | 80.0 | 63.8 | 76.8 | 78.2 | 82.9 | 91.5 | 117.2 | 90.7 | 65.4 | 45.5 | 65.1 | 67.7 | 79.3 | 101.9 |
| December. | 108.7 | 90.4 | 78.9 | 63.9 | 74.1 | 77.3 | 81.9 | 92.2 | 111.5 | 85.7 | 65.5 | 45.5 | 63.1 | 66.4 | 80.0 | 104.0 |

## Census of Manufacturers: 1935*

*Summary for Maryland*

The statement below gives summary figures for 1935 for the State of Maryland compiled from data collected in the Manufactures Census taken this year, with comparative figures for 1933 and 1929. (The Census of Manufactures covers the printing and publishing industries as well as manufacturing industries proper.) All figures for 1935 are preliminary and subject to revision.

(Because they account for a negligible portion of the national output, plants with annual production valued under $5,000 have been excluded since 1919.)

| | 1935 | 1933 | 1929 | Percent of increase or decrease (−) | |
|---|---|---|---|---|---|
| | | | | 1933–1935 | 1929–1935 |
| Number of establishments. | 2,697 | 2,476 | 3,210 | 8.9 | −16.0 |
| Wage earners (average for the year (a) | 119,903 | 100,236 | 130,896 | 19.6 | − 8.4 |
| Wages (b) | $111,303,193 | $ 82,563,281 | $ 148,598,057 | 34.8 | −25.1 |
| Cost of materials, containers for products, fuel and purchased electric energy (b) | 441,146,873 | 278,374,077 | 689,248,533 | 58.5 | −36.0 |
| Value of products (b) | 755,843,200 | 518,707,419 | 1,108,721,014 | 45.7 | −31.8 |
| Value added by manufacture (c) | 314,696,327 | 240,333,342 | 419,472,481 | 30.9 | −25.0 |

(a) Not including salaried officers and employees. The item for wage-earners is an average of the numbers reported for the several months of the year. In calculating it, equal weight must be given to full-time and part-time wage-earners (not reported separately by the manufacturers), and for this reason it exceeds the number that would have been required to perform the work done in manufacturing and printing and publishing industries if all wage-earners had been continuously employed throughout the year. The quotient obtained by dividing the amount of wages by the average number of wage-earners cannot, therefore, be accepted as representing the average wage received by full-time wage-earners. In making comparisons between the figures for 1935 and those for earlier years, the possibility that the proportion of part-time employment varied from year to year should be taken into account.

(b) Profits or losses cannot be calculated from the Census figures because no data are collected for certain expense items, such as interest, rent, depreciation, taxes, insurance, and advertising.

(c) Value of products less cost of materials, containers, fuel, and purchased electric energy.

* Preliminary report of the Bureau of the Census, United States Department of Commerce, Washington, D. C., released January 18, 1937.

## DIVISION OF BOILER INSPECTION

The State Boiler Inspectors maintain a State-wide inspection service, making the initial inspection of all power boilers installed in the State of Maryland and annual inspection of all power boilers in the City of Baltimore, with the exception of boilers now insured and regularly inspected by an authorized insurance company. This division also cooperates with the Examiners of Stationary Engineers in the enforcement of their law in Baltimore City. Several hundred complaints and investigations were handled during the course of the year.

The danger from explosions has been definitely minimized by the requirements of the Boiler Inspection law. In the past year, explosions occurred in only three cases; one cast iron heating boiler, one cast iron hot water supply boiler, and one air tank (unfired pressure vessel). All three vessels were obsolete. Since January 1932 only two high pressure boiler explosions have occurred and both boilers were installed and operated without notification of and inspection by this division.

The adoption of the codes of the American Society of Mechanical Engineers for the construction and installation of steam generating plants and equipment has been an important factor in protecting the lives and property of the people of Maryland. Another important safeguard is the law which applies to Baltimore City requiring the operation of steam boilers by licensed engineers who, in order to obtain licenses, must meet certain qualifications.

It has been the practice of owners during the past few years to continue the use of old equipment as long as possible to avoid the expense of replacement. Wherever possible this division has cooperated in such instances, but it was necessary in 1936 to condemn and forbid the use of 8 steam boilers and orders have been issued to remove 25 more from further service.

During the year 1936 this division inspected 362 boilers, 309 of which were large boilers and 53 of which were miniatures, and 10 unfired pressure vessels. Of the boilers, 144 were located in the various counties and 218 in Baltimore City. There is a charge of $5.00 for inspecting each boiler and vessel and issuing Certificate of Inspection, and for boiler inspections in the counties an additional charge of actual expenses incurred is made. During the year $1,860.00 was collected and deposited to the account of the State Treasurer from this source and an additional $5.00 was collected on inspection of a condemned boiler. There was no charge made for inspection of three boilers located at State institutions. This division also collected

$851.00 in taxes from insurance companies for boilers insured in Baltimore City. Ten insurance company boiler inspectors were commissioned to inspect boilers in the State of Maryland, from which an additional revenue of $50.00 was derived.

## REPORT OF BUREAU OF MINES

The business of coal mining in Western Maryland during the calendar year 1936 was not very greatly different from that of the year 1935. During the first half of the year the larger coal companies worked fairly well but most of the small mines were idle. Up to the end of the year, during the winter months there was considerable demand for domestic coal and the smaller mines worked every day. The demand for coal by trucks at the small mines was unusually insistent and continuous. In the summer and early fall one of the larger companies continued to operate continuously but some of the others worked only the leadings to provide development for the coming winter. In the early fall for a short time there was a scarcity of railroad cars and this interfered somewhat with production.

During July there was labor trouble at the mine of one company but the mine was idle for only one week or so, and the difficulty was soon remedied. Labor troubles in Cumberland, in the early winter, lessened the demand for steam coal to some extent and this resulted in some slack time operation in mines adjacent to Cumberland.

There was very little demand for coal for export, but the increased demand for steam coal, as a result of the revival of work in the steel industry, caused a sudden sharp demand for coke, and many beehive ovens in Pennsylvania and West Virginia were again put in blast. Some of these ovens had had no coal since 1929. A great deal of this demand was due to the fact that by-product oven coke was being used in steel manufacture and the domestic markets, which had heretofore been supplied by by-product sized coke, had to be supplied from beehive ovens.

Experiments were made in coking the slack coal from the Bakerstown seam in southern Georges Creek in bee-hive coke ovens in Pennsylvania and West Virginia plants. This experimental work is still under way.

Many improvements in mining methods and in mining equipment were made during the year and also a few mines improved their method of cleaning and preparing coal.

One company continued the practice of stocking coal which was begun in 1935; apparently this has been a success. The larger users of coal, in Cumberland and vicinity, have continued to stock a considerable quantity of coal at their power plants.

Some new mines of small capacity have recently resumed work. Some of these are entirely new operations; others were old operations which had been lying idle for six or eight years, but have been put in operation again as a result of the demand for domestic coal.

## STAFF OF THE STATE COMMISSIONER OF LABOR AND STATISTICS

| Name | Address | Title |
|---|---|---|
| Henry Lay Duer | Baltimore | Commissioner |
| Margaret W. Hatfield, | Baltimore | Chief Clerk |
| Madeleine V. Dunne | Baltimore | Statistician |
| Mary M. Wootton | Baltimore | Supervisor, Special Permits |
| Dr. Henry Sheppard | Baltimore | Medical Examiner |
| Dr. Wright S. Sudler | Baltimore | Medical Examiner |
| Lynn M. Cave | Baltimore | Boiler Inspector |
| A. Dewey Webster | Baltimore | Boiler Inspector |
| William D. Bloom | Catonsville | Inspector |
| Harry A. LeBrun | Towson | Inspector |
| Robert C. Bedford | Halethorpe | Inspector |
| John F. Duggan | Baltimore | Inspector |
| William H. Fox | Baltimore | Inspector |
| Lewis B. Francis | Salisbury | Inspector |
| Benjamin C. Green | Towson | Inspector |
| George H. McCauley | Baltimore | Inspector |
| Edith S. Maynard | Baltimore | Inspector |
| Monica McCarthy | Baltimore | Inspector |
| Joseph F. Miller | Baltimore | Inspector |
| Edmund Rawa | Baltimore | Inspector |
| Barclay E. Tucker | Forest Hill | Inspector |
| Arthur I. Williams | Halethorpe | Inspector |
| Catherine B. Hughes | Baltimore | Senior Clerk |
| Elizabeth Sanders | Baltimore | Senior Clerk |
| Selma B. Cone | Baltimore | Stenographer-Secretary |
| Margaret C. Slimmer | Baltimore | Senior Stenographer |
| Mary K. Schelle | Baltimore | Senior Stenographer |
| Bessie F. Robinson | Baltimore | Junior Stenographer |
| Margaret D. Kach | Baltimore | Junior Typist |
| Essie R. Levin | Baltimore | Junior Typist |
| Mary F. Riley | Baltimore | Junior Typist |

## Bureau of Mines

| | | |
|---|---|---|
| John J. Rutledge | Baltimore | Chief Mine Engineer |
| Frank T. Powers | Frostburg | Inspector |
| Clyde J. Rowe | Westernport | Inspector |
| Julia E. Jefferson | Baltimore | Clerk-Stenographer |
| Sarah Borinsky | | Clerk |

Lightning Source UK Ltd.
Milton Keynes UK
UKHW050011080119
334942UK00006BA/233/P